I0475897

# Mastering Flash

## with

# Fujifilm X Cameras

"PROFESSIONAL INSIGHTS FOR EXPERIENCED PHOTOGRAPHERS"

Version 1.0

ISBN 978-1-312-70725-2

Published by The Friedman Archives Press

## GRATITUDE

I would like to thank the following for their invaluable contributions to the quality of this undertaking:

Justin Moriarty                                    Fujifilm Australia

And further thanks to my models, Jayne, Levi, Beth, Ben, Sarah, Sarah, Lincoln, Steven, Sophie, Serena, Mariah, Raylee and Steve.


## FOR THOSE OF YOU WHO BOUGHT THE PRINTED B&W OR E-READER VERSION

The price of the printed books come with a free, full-color .pdf version of the book. Just send an email to info@FriedmanArchives.com. Attach the receipt of the book you bought (if you didn't buy it from the FriedmanArchivesPress.com website, then Friedman Archives does not have your customer information), and we'll send you a download link. (The same thing goes for those who bought this book as a B&W e-reader.)


## ANDROID AND IOS READERS

If you are reading the .pdf version of this e-book on an Android or iOS platform, your reading experience might be enhanced if you viewed the .pdf file via one of these free apps:

- For iOS: GoodReader from www.goodreader.net
- For Android: ezyPDF Reader (from the Google Play store)


All Fujifilm content used with permission. Thank you.

## THE AUTHOR

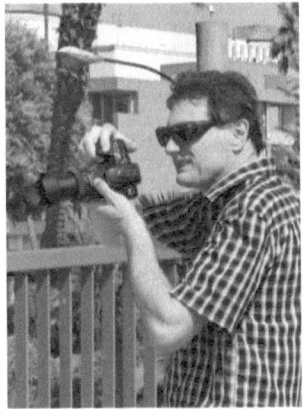

**Tony** is a photographer, author, pilot, teacher, and lecturer, and has a passion for photography. He conducts photographic seminars teaching the fundamentals of digital photography through to advanced lighting.

*"Anyone can learn to take great pictures if they have the desire."* And, it is not so much the equipment (though it is important), as the *person*, that makes those pictures great.

Tony is widely travelled, a businessman and entrepenuer. He spends much of his time writing, teaching, travelling, lecturing, and hunting great images.

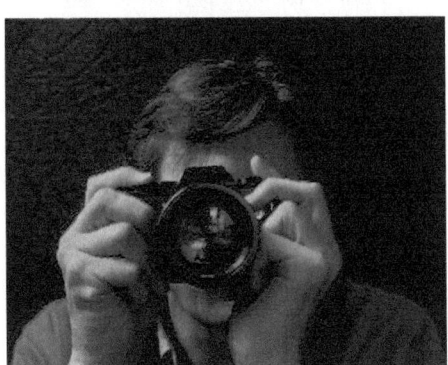

Visit   www.TonyPhillips.org   to learn more. Or email Tony at Info@TonyPhillips.org.

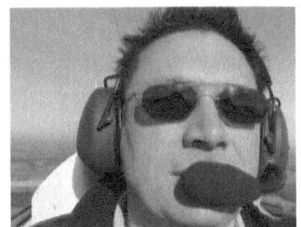

Some of Tony's other photography books.

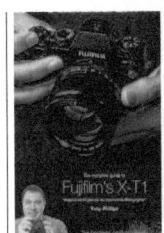
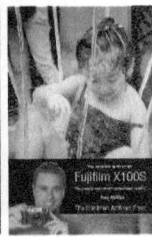
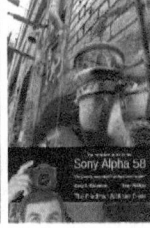
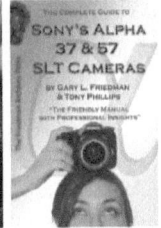
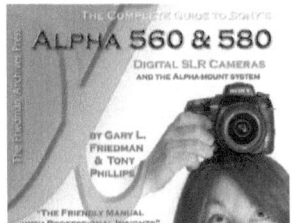

# TABLE OF CONTENTS

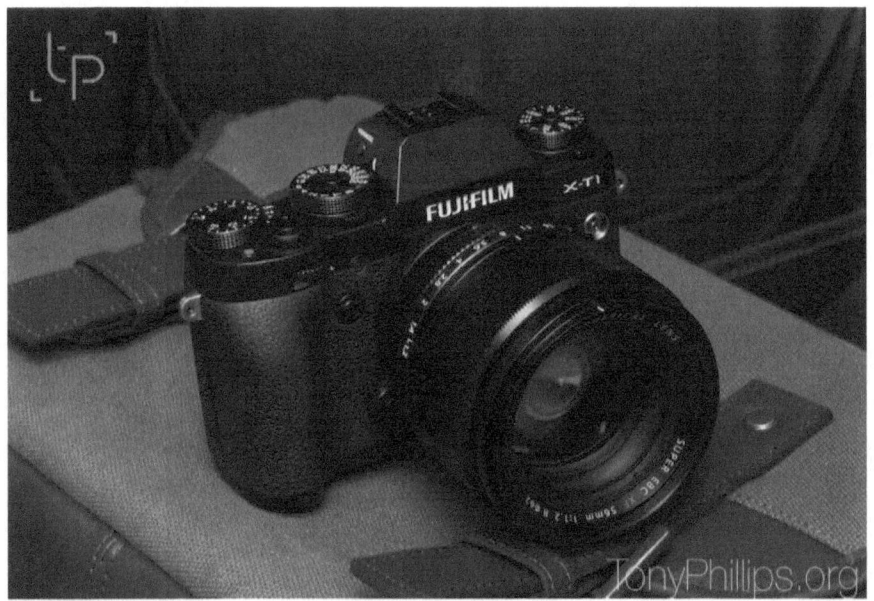

*Lighting for desire...*

# THIS BOOK

The *only* reason to use flash is to bring light to a composition in just the quality, strength, and location *you* want – to create the result you are looking for. Flash is an extension of our use and understanding of light, which is fundamentally what photography is about.

This book is for anyone who wants to improve their use of flash – both on and off the camera. The tools and techniques discussed apply equally to shooting snapshots, weddings, portraits, travel – in fact any photography where changing the quality of light gets you the desired outcome.

This book discusses:
- Fujifilm X-platform flash modes;
- Fujifilm and third-party flash units;
- TTL (automatic) flash;
- On-camera flash;
- Wireless (off-camera) flash;
- Wireless triggers;
- Light modifiers (umbrellas, softboxes, reflectors);
- Ratio lighting;
- Using flash for portraits and studio work;
- Mastering manual flash so you feel comfortable using it anywhere, at any time; and
- Real High Speed Sync for X100 series cameras.

In addition, there are appendices covering:
- The Histogram, and how to use it for perfect flash exposure; and
- A Condensed Guide to the basics of Exposure, and the exposure variables.

The information in this book covers the use of flash with all current "X" cameras including the XE, XT, and X Pro series of interchangeable lens cameras, as well as the unique real high speed flash sync capability available in fixed lens X100/S/T leaf shutter cameras.

The reason many people struggle with getting flash to work well is that cameras do *NOT* think about light the same way you or I do. Of course, we understand this – but applying that understanding to flash can be a challenge because flash is so transitory.

In this book, I aim to peel back the layers, to demystify and simplify flash. I encourage you to use flash everywhere. Indeed, professional photographers use flash in many, many images that don't look "flash lit" at all. It's part of what makes their "wow" photos so appealing.

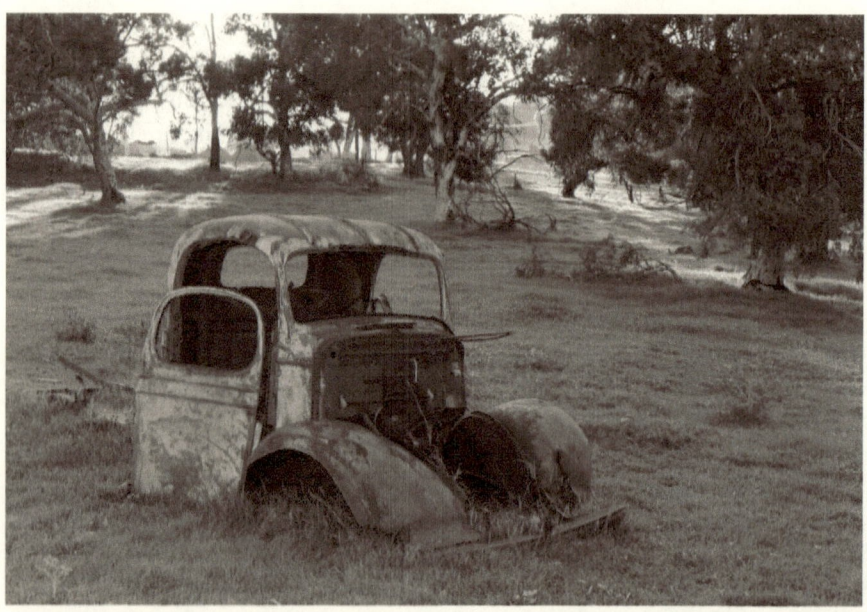

*Figure 0-1:* *This image required a high-powered wireless flash to lift the wreck against the setting sun. Velvia film helped pop the colour just a bit under the deep shade blanketing most of the scene.*

Unlike some of my previous books, in this book I make the assumption you're an experienced photographer with a solid grasp on the basics (ISO, f/stop, shutter speed). I do include an appendix on this for reference though.

With this in mind, let's jump right in to advanced lighting, and how to use flash with Fujifilm X-platform cameras to get the image you are aiming for.

# CHAPTER 1 WHY LEARN LIGHTING?

Why spend time learning about lighting? I mean, you have one of the best low-light cameras on the planet. And everyone knows using wireless flash with "X" "cameras means you are in manual flash mode. So why do it?

It would be this!

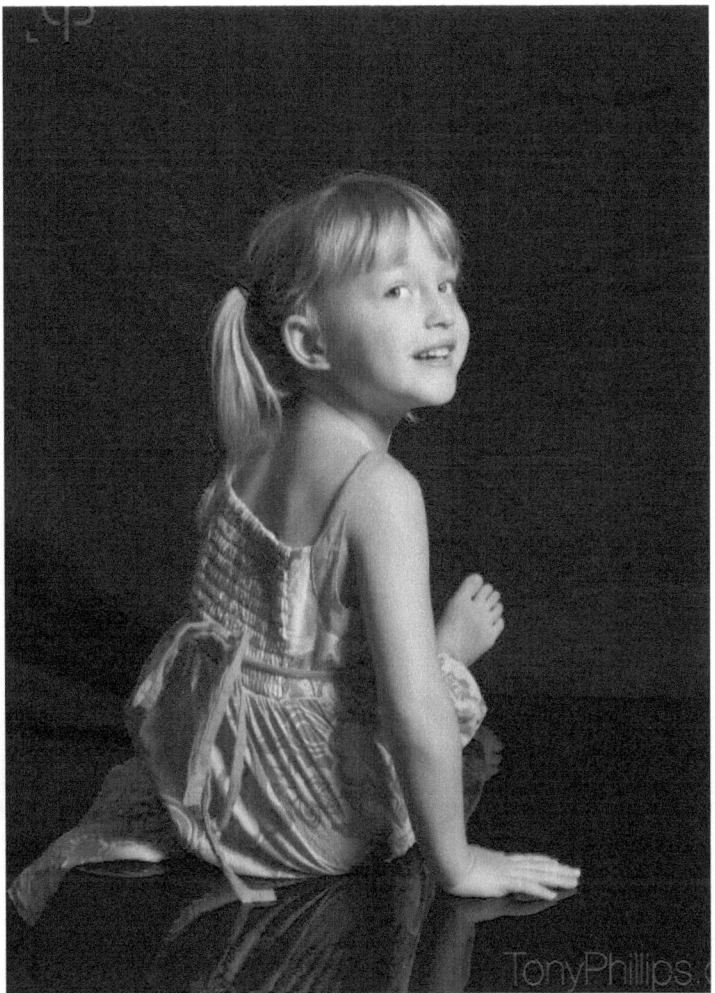

**Figure 1-1** *Get lighting right, and you can wait till "the look" comes along.*

For many people, adding an accessory flash to their camera is about getting *more* light. And frequently it stays atop the camera, sometimes pointed at a ceiling or wall for a bounce effect. But that's as far as it goes.

Yet photography is about the *quality* of light. It's about telling a story *written in light*, and frozen in time by your camera's sensor when you press the shutter button.

The topics in this book are therefore about the quality of light – and how you achieve a desired outcome with the tools at hand.

Flash is a lighting tool at your disposal to write light to suit your own story. If you have an appetite to write strong light-stories, then perhaps some of the techniques discussed herein will help you do just that.

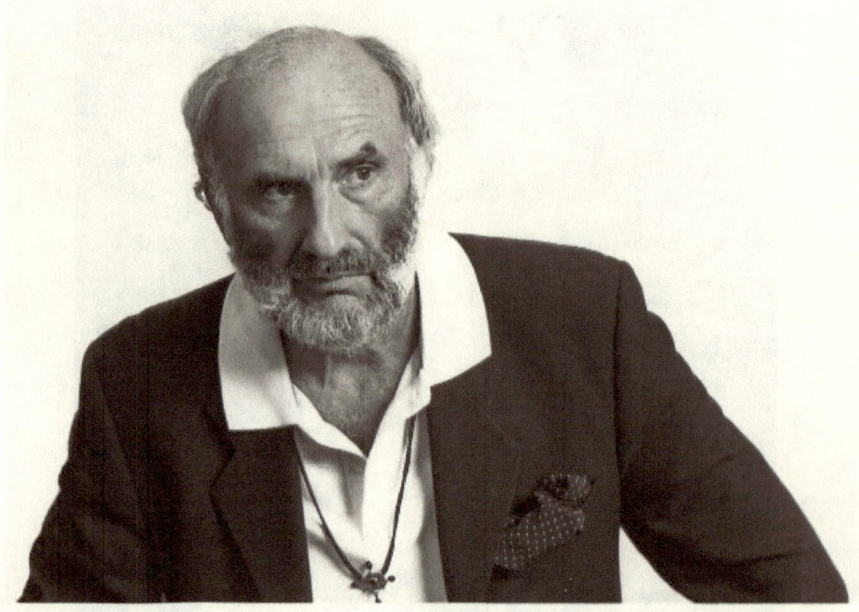

**Figure 1-2:** *Flash and a High Contrast Monochrome process gives this portrait the "Hemmingway" look.*

While most of the material in the following pages is applicable to virtually any camera, and specifically applicable to all interchangeable X-platform cameras, the X100/S/T leaf shutter cameras have a special ability to master light in a way virtually no other camera can, due to their ability to use flash at quite high shutter speeds. And while real high speed sync has been around for quite a while now in other leaf shutter lenses (at a steep cost), this technique is now readily, and cost-effectively available for anyone wishing to add a highly-desirable photographic outcome to their own light story.

So if you own one of these cameras, there are sections in this book specific to the use of flash, RHSS (real high speed sync), the leaf shutter, and ND filter of the X100/S/T cameras.

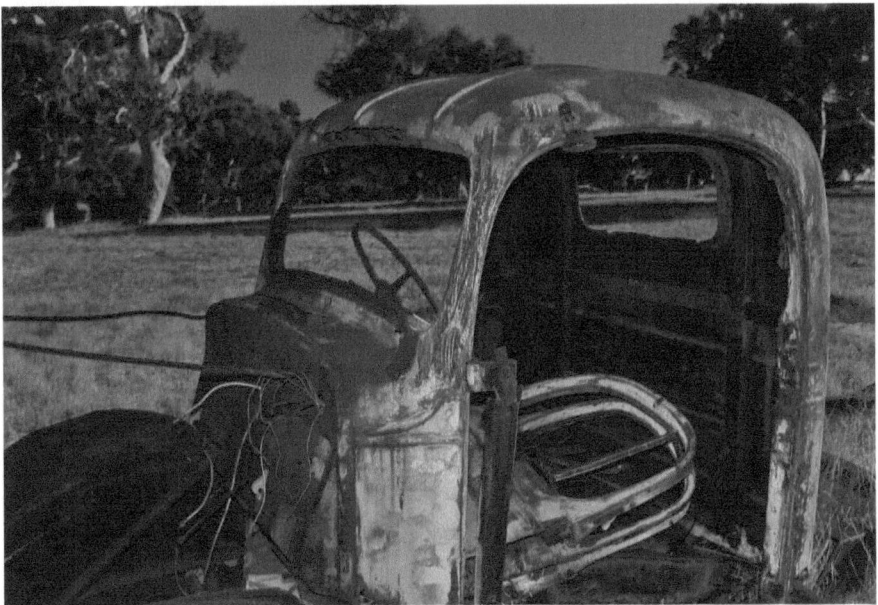

**Figure 1-3:** *Expect this from your X100/S/T!*

*Real High Speed flash Sync gives "Wow!" photos like this right out of the camera. (1/1000$^{th}$, F/2, Velvia film simulation, EF-X20 flash, 100° summer sun.)*

All "X" cameras are fun, lightweight cameras for everyday use. In the following pages I will show you not only how to master and manage flash exposure, but the kind of kit you can take with you on your travels that will keep your luggage light, yet give maximum creativity in your use of lighting.

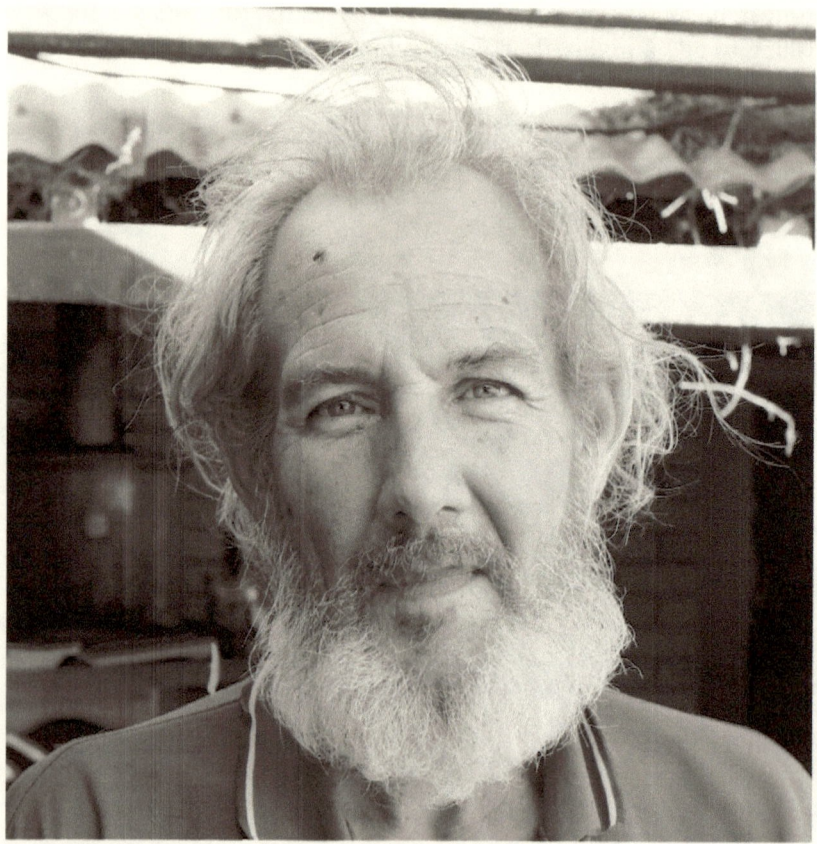

**Figure 1-4:** *Great lighting does not require mountains of gear. One camera, one flash and a trigger is all the kit you need. The rest is up to you.*

# CHAPTER 2    LIGHT

## HOW CAMERAS THINK ABOUT LIGHT

The reason many people struggle with getting flash right is that cameras do *NOT* think about light the same way you do. So let's spend a few minutes considering how a camera understands light. Of course, if you know all this, just skip ahead.

Our eyes are a marvel current photographic technology is nowhere near matching. I mean, how many times have you taken a picture and the outcome is way brighter, or way darker than *you* see the scene? Quite a few, right?

It's one of the challenges of being a photographer. You are creating images with light, with tools that just *don't see light the way you do*. So understanding *how* cameras see light, and *how* to get them to see light the way you want them to is part of the fun – and the challenge.

This all has to do with the notion of dynamic range. The dynamic range of your eyes, for instance, is about 30 stops of light! Digital camera sensors on the other hand, master only 8 stops or so. So no wonder you see what they don't "see".

This is important to understand. If you metered for the scene in **Figure 2-1**, and you required 1/1000$^{th}$ of a second (shutter speed) for correct exposure of the brightest parts of the image, then 8 stops less than that means the darkest parts will only yield detail if you can properly expose them with 1/4 second shutter speed (8 stops away). That same 8 stop range for your eyes is a doddle. You see detail in the very brightest part of the scene, and many, many stops below where your camera has given up and rendered everything black.

And the odd part is, while we can take multiple pictures and turn them into true HDR (high dynamic range) images, they seem quite fake to our eye. This clearly has to do with the way our brain processes these inputs.

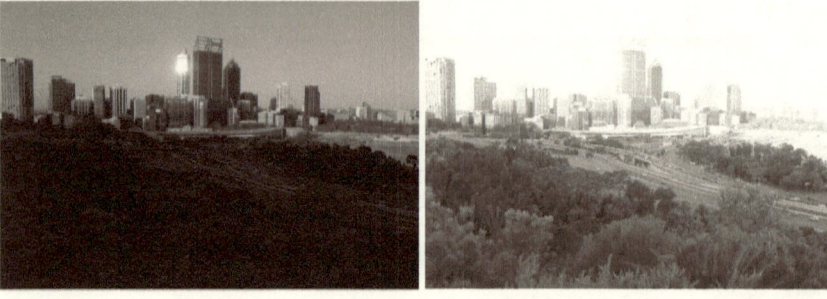

**Figure 2-1:** *Cameras can expose for light, or dark, but not both - the sky, or the foreground (in this case). What I saw when I took these pictures was neither of these scenes. Rather something more of a blend. You have to deliberately meter for the darks to get the image on the right. Your camera's exposure algorithms will never want to take this kind of picture.*

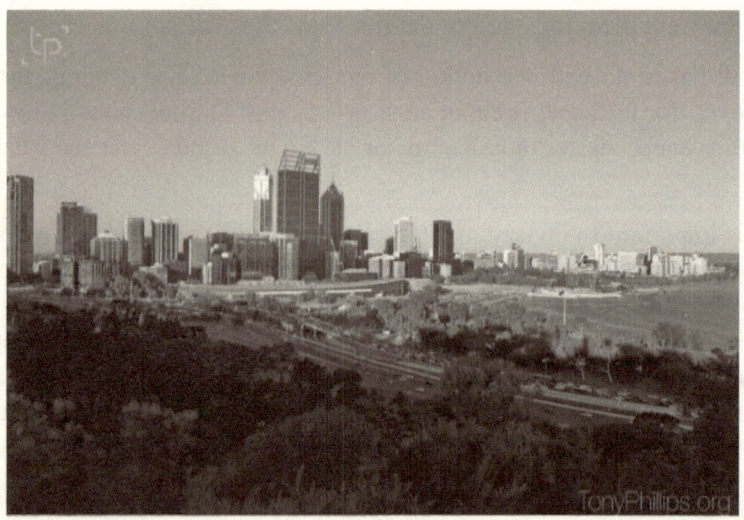

**Figure 2-2:**   *This is an* **attempt** *to depict the scene as I saw it. And even this is not right. To add back the dark detail I could easily see simply makes the picture seem flat and bizarre.*

This huge dynamic range difference between eye and camera is one of the reasons to use forced (fill) flash, even on a bright, sunny day (or especially on a bright sunny day), to lift detail in shadows so you capture a scene more the way your eye sees it. This is part of the reason X100/S/T RHSS (real high speed sync) flash photography appeals to me too. It gives me back richness and detail (the experience) I perceived I was having while I was in the scene shooting.

In order to determine what exposure to use for a picture (let's assume we are in Program Exposure mode for the time being), cameras use internal metering functions to measure the available light – whether it comes from ambient lighting (either natural or artificial), or flash.

## MEASURING LIGHT – REFLECTANCE VS INCIDENCE

At one time though, camera's *did not* have sophisticated exposure meters in them, and the only way to ensure correct exposure was via a (far less sophisticated version) of the handheld exposure meter shown in **Figure 2-3**. This meter measures the amount falling on a subject. Tell it what ISO and f/stop you want to use, and it will tell you what shutter speed will give you accurate exposure. It works for flash too, and once you understand it, it's always right, and quite easy to use.

This kind of meter works differently to the one you have in your camera though. The camera can only measure light *reflecting back to it* from your subject. On the other hand, the handheld meter measures exposure at the subject (*light hitting the subject*). Now this might sound like the same thing, but it is not.

Reflectance metering (like your camera does) is influenced by the colour of clothing, skin, image background, reflective quality of fabrics and so on. If you've ever shot a wedding you'll know that white wedding dresses reflect more light than dark suits, causing a real bother for your camera's metering system. The same is true if you attempt to shoot a portrait with a predominantly white building (church say), as your background. Let the camera have its head, and it will *never* come out white – the way your eye sees it. Yet despite these obvious limitations, it's tremendously convenient to have a metering system built into your camera. And in truth, for so many circumstances, reflectance (in-camera) metering works rather well. It's just where things get tricky that you see its limitations, and might benefit from more knowledge and possibly another metering system.

Incidence metering (like the handheld meter does) only measures the amount of light arriving at the subject, ignoring all of the above distractions. It is only interested in the *light* right at the point you want to photograph. Stand a charcoal suit beside a white wedding dress, and the meter gets it right every time! Even when you are using flash as all, or part of your lighting source.

So which is the best kind of metering to use? And the answer is, it depends…

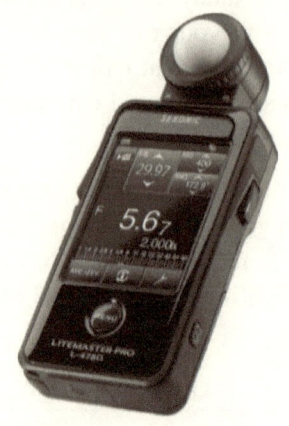

*Figure 2-3: This is a thoroughly new (yet old-fashioned) exposure meter. They're becoming popular again because they serve a very useful purpose: Used correctly they always give you the correct exposure recommendation, regardless of how dark or how light your subject is, what colour it is, or what the surrounding background or lighting is. An exposure meter takes the guesswork out of shooting in manual flash mode.*

If you think about it, a camera actually has no idea what it is looking at. It doesn't understand yellow or green, black or white, or the reflective properties of a huge array of viscose fabrics. And given the complexity of the idea of reflective metering, it's amazing it works so well.

The secret to maximizing its use lies in understanding the underlying assumption about what makes a proper exposure "proper" – and the simplified answer is that the camera's metering system has been programmed to assume that *ALL* subjects are 18% grey!

If you look at a greyscale chart, you'll see that 18% is almost exactly half way between black and white (on the chart). And analyzing the reflectance of thousands of pictures also shows that *on average, they are 18% grey too* (see **Figure 2-4**). So, since cameras use reflective metering, they are programmed to view the *exposure* of the world this way. They think that the average brightness of everything is 18% (on that greyscale chart).

This applies to all images, no matter the lighting source – flash, ambient, sunlight. So understanding this will help you achieve good results when you choose to shoot with flash as either a fill, or main light source.

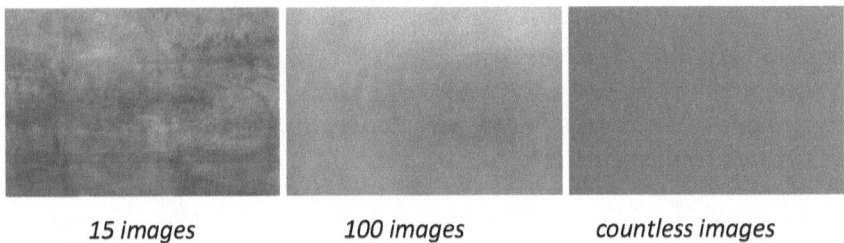

| 15 images | 100 images | countless images |

**Figure 2-4:** *When you average together hundreds and thousands of normal photographs, you will eventually end up with an image that's 18% grey. That's because "average" images reflect back about 18% of the light. Your camera is programmed to expose for average images, and that's why it always assumes that the reflected light it sees must be rendered at 18% brightness (grey) to give a "proper" exposure.*

Once you know this, it explains why there are situations where your camera never gets exposure right at all (with, or without flash). When it's looking at something which is pure white, for instance, it's still programmed to think it's really 18% grey. Same is true for pure black. **Figure 2-5** and **Figure 2-6** shows you what I mean – and you can easily demonstrate this yourself by taking a picture of something which is all white in normal daylight. Follow that up with another which is all black, and most remarkably, black looks grey, and so does white! Once you know this of course, you'll also be able to take steps to correct it.

Notwithstanding this limitation, this understanding of the 18% grey principle is what makes reflectance metering in cameras possible, and it works in most situations, giving results most of us are happy with most of the time.

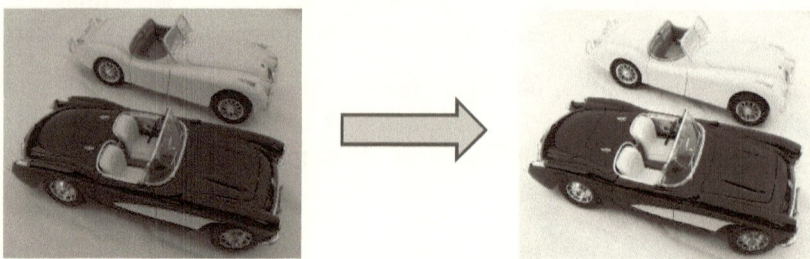

***Figure 2-5***: ***Top Left***: *The background for this image was actually bright white. And the scene was well lit. But notice how the camera's exposure metering obeys its programing to make things look 18% grey.* ***Top Right***: *See how easy this is to alter with exposure compensation (+1.7ev in this case).*

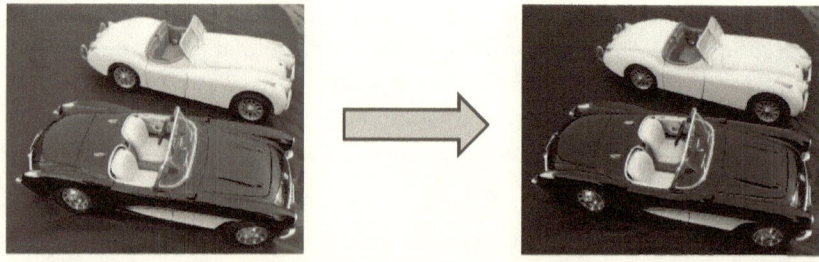

***Figure 2-6***: *The situation is the same when the background is black.* ***Left***: *The camera still tries to make everything look 18% grey!* ***Right***: *Easily fixed with exposure compensations (-1.3ev). Of course, if I'd used a handheld incidence exposure meter these images would have been accurately exposed first time.*
*All these images were shot outdoors with natural ambient lighting in open shade.*

---

***TIP***: *To make whites white again, simply increase exposure compensation. You are effectively overexposing so white will be less-18% grey. To get blacks blacker, do the opposite, and underexpose to make them less grey (more black).*

*Knowing this design limitation, and using the camera's inbuilt compensation tool is a small price to pay for the convenience of having a great metering system built right into the camera.*

---

So far, we've examined how cameras think about light, and how that differs from the human eye. Of course, while we haven't got to it yet, adding flash to the lighting equation obviously changes exposure. Yet the principles are the same. Left to its own devices, the camera always makes choices about how much to expose a scene based on these limitations and "rules".

Switch flash on, and these "rules" extend to the flash exposure too. Which accounts for why flash-lit subjects don't always appear the way you saw them (or want them to look). Switch flash to manual, and you are on your own with exposure. Which, as it turns out, is not that bad a place to be.

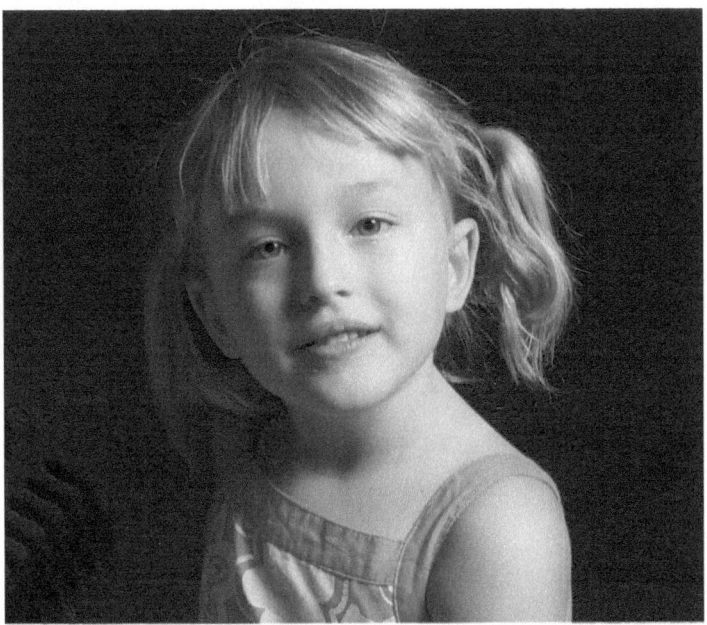

*Figure 2-7:* *Once your exposure is set, if the distance between your model and the light source does not change, there is no need to meter for flash between shots. Just shoot away as the shot presents itself. See Chapter 8 for more.*

# CHAPTER 3     FLASH MODES

All X-platform cameras have automatic, and semi-automatic flash exposure modes, as well as manual flash mode which requires you to manage flash exposure yourself.

Indeed, if you want to get the flash off the camera for more dramatic effects, manual flash is likely to become your friend, since the only way to use the TTL (auto flash) modes with the flash removed from the camera, is to connect it via cable.

But don't let this concern you. Once you reach the end of this book, I hope you are freely experimenting with both manual, and off-camera flash, to great effect.

X-platform flash modes are accessible via the Menu, the Q-Menu, or a dedicated or programmed function button.

Flash mode selection is generally only available when shooting Single Frame still images, and whilst shooting Multiple Exposures.

Let's briefly examine each of the X-platform's flash modes:

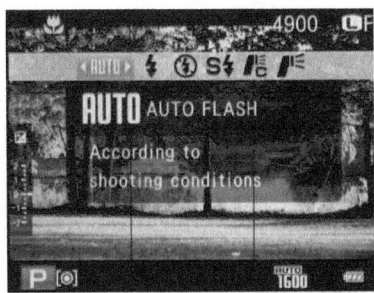

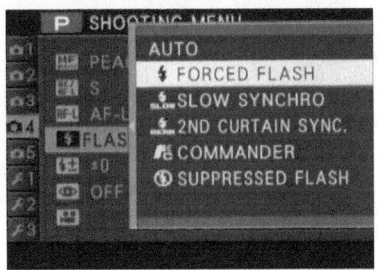

*Figure 3-1:* The flash modes. **Top:** Some X cameras display these icons on the screen when you press the Flash function button. **Bottom:** The flash modes menu is difficult to get to. Fortunately we have the Q-Menu, or on most "X" cameras you can program a function button.

## SUPPRESSED FLASH

Suppressed = Off. What else is there to say? Well, given the usual connotations (go ahead, look it up), it's a strange choice of word for "Off". You won't need to "suppress" flash if you engage the camera's "Silent" Mode. Silent Mode prevents the flash from firing.

## AUTO FLASH

In Auto Flash mode the camera decides whether to use the flash or not, and when it decides to do so it behaves according to the "Forced Flash" behavior described next.

Of note: "Auto" is only available when in Program exposure mode (Shutter and Aperture both on "A"). So if you can't see it, this may be the reason.

## FORCED FLASH

Forced Flash is also described as "fill flash" in various "X" camera manuals – and I really wish they'd called it that. But no matter what it's named, the entire "X" range has one of the best implementations of "fill-flash" I've used.

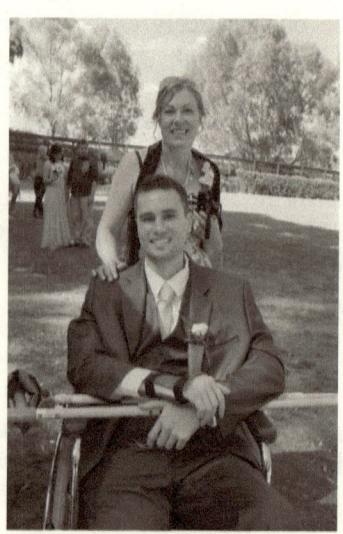

Ordinarily cameras expect their flash must provide all the light needed to properly expose the scene. If you were in a dark restaurant this makes sense – though given the nature of light fall-off, the outcome is usually some brightly lit subjects sans friends and all background atmosphere. Fill flash works differently. The truth is, we frequently take pictures in situations where there is other light (often the sun, or significant artificial light). In this circumstance the camera's Forced

**Figure 3-2:**   *Outdoor portrait with "fill" flash. Notice how it lifts the shadows which would otherwise spoil the shot.*

Flash mode acts as a fill light, only outputting enough to brighten the shadows (see **Figure 3-2**) and enhance the overall exposure.

Forced Flash switches between these two modalities as needed. So, take a picture in that darkened restaurant and your camera will attempt to light the whole scene itself, step outside in the bright sunlight with the same flash setting to brighten shadows, giving them back their detail.

In fact, outside in bright daylight is one of the best times to use forced (fill) flash. For example, in **Figure 3-2**, the background was so bright that it threatened to underexpose my subjects. Of course, given my eye can see far more dynamic range than the camera, everything looked OK to me. Yet I could tell from the shadows that flash was required to give me a *picture* that looked OK too.

---

*X100/S/T leaf shutter users:*

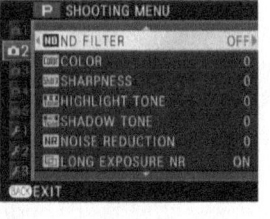

*Combine Forced Flash with the use of the in-camera Neutral Density (ND) filter and the real high speed syncing capability provided by the X100/S/T's leaf shutter, and you have what so few other photographers have; a camera that excels outdoors in bright conditions.*

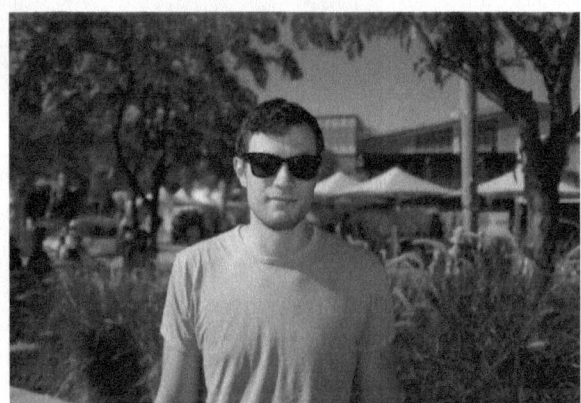

*The ND Filter can be combined with a high shutter speed (1/1000th in this case) to cut bright ambient daylight yet use a wide aperture. Add "Forced" (fill) flash with the onboard or accessory flash (I used the EF-X20 atop the camera) to light the foreground and make the subject pop. Even snapshots like this take on a more magical extra-dimensionality.*

---

There's only one difference between Auto and Forced Flash. In Auto mode, the camera decides if it will fire the flash. Forced Flash means you are "forcing" it to fire when you take a picture. But even so, it will try to get the exposure right as we just discovered.

## SLOW SYNCHRO

This *is* the restaurant/party flash mode! It's intended to "burn in" background light (by slowing the shutter speed to near what it would be if you were taking a picture without the flash). Your subject is lit with flash – thereby eliminating the "bright faces in a pool of black" these situations produce. This is often called "dragging the shutter", since shutter speed is usually way too low to capture anything other than a blurry picture, and you are *counting* on the flash pulse to "freeze" your subject, making them sharp in the image (See **Figure 3-3**).

Mind you, shutter speeds can be quite low – so beware of movement in your intended image. In an informal "Slow Synchro" Flash test, I notice the "X" cameras want $1/30^{th}$ of a second with Forced flash, $1/10^{th}$ with Suppressed Flash, and $1/10^{th}$ with Slow Synchro flash.

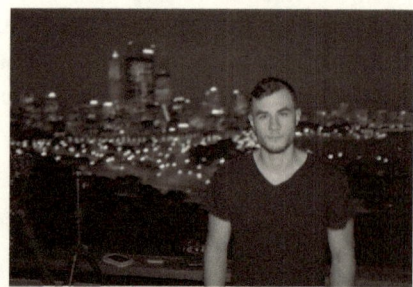

Given the X-platform's generally excellent high ISO, low-light capability, Slow Synchro actually becomes quite useful. It's not only useful indoors, but works well to light subjects in situations like **Figure 3-3** after sunset. Experiment

*Figure 3-3: Slow Synchro can bring ambience back to your evening images. (Untouched X100S JPEG.)*

with it for a while and you'll find yourself using it more and more.

Slow synchro is only available in Program or Aperture Exposure modes since the camera *must* slow shutter speed sufficiently to gather background light. In practice, the ambient light can be fairly low, and you will still get a result.

## SECOND CURTAIN SYNC.

2<sup>nd</sup> Curtain Sync, also known as rear-curtain sync acts a lot like normal forced flash, or slow synchro, but with one big difference. In those flash modes, the flash fires at the *beginning* of the exposure. Second curtain sync fires the flash at the *end* of the exposure, just before the shutter closes.

Now at first blush, this might not seem too big a deal. But what this lets you do is control trailing light (vs leading light) when you're using flash with:

   a) Moving subjects, *and*
   b) Long shutter speeds (to collect ambient background light).

And what this does is easily seen in **Figure 3-4** where we capture motion blur with ambient light *and* freeze our subject in the picture with the flash.

What's happening here is that normal Forced Flash, (or Slow Synchro flash) freezes the subject by firing at the beginning of the long exposure. But the long shutter speed continues to capture light until the shutter finally closes – giving us a subsequent light (motion) trail ahead of the main subject – which just looks odd. Second Curtain Sync freezes the subject at the end of the exposure, meaning the motion-trail is behind them where it seems sensible for it to be.

Second Curtain Sync is not currently available on all X-platform cameras.

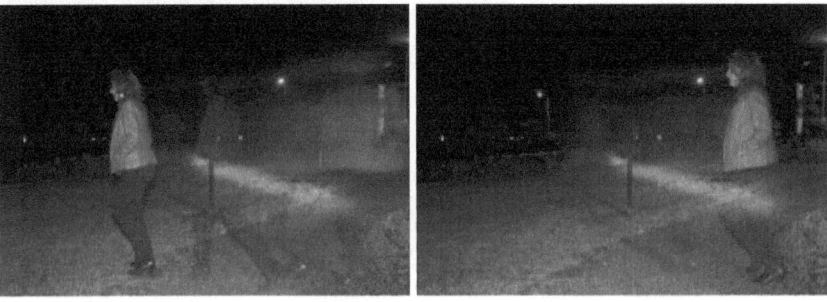

*Figure 3-4: Left: Second curtain flash puts the motion-trail behind a moving subject where we expect it to be. Right: Normal flash does just the opposite in this scenario. Both images used the same exposure settings. Only the flash mode changed. Shutter speed = 1.5 seconds in this case.*

---

*TTL (an acronym for Through The Lens) means the camera is metering both the ambient and flash light through the camera lens (as the flash is firing), and automatically managing the amount of flash required to deliver what the camera considers is a correct exposure given the selected flash mode. We will investigate this in more depth later in the book.*

---

While all preceding flash modes are automatic/semi-automatic TTL modes, the following are manual modes, requiring you to select the amount of power to use to produce the desired exposure.

## COMMANDER (WIRELESS FLASH)

Commander Flash mode is designed around one simple concept: pictures often look much more dramatic and professional if the light is coming from someplace *OTHER* than where the camera is.

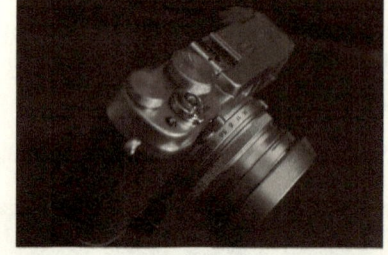

In the past this involved wires – which you can still do – but now you can go wireless, and put the flash virtually anywhere you want (with caveats), and it will fire as though it was still on the camera – alas *not* with TTL automatic exposure though! (See **Figure 3-5.**)

*Figure 3-5: A self-referential sample of a "Commander" wireless flash image. With the flash off-camera, you can produce selective shadows and highlights giving dramatic results!*

In Commander mode the inbuilt (or Fujifilm accessory flash) fires a burst of light to instruct the off-camera flash(es) (there can be more than one) when to fire.

At this stage, the EF-X20 is the only Fujifilm accessory flash you can use in Commander mode (either on or off the camera), but I expect that will change in the relatively near future.

This is such an important and useful feature that I have dedicated an extended section to it later in this book. My hope is that Chapter 7 will give you a taste of the possibilities that wireless flash offers you (and how to use it).

## EXTERNAL FLASH

Some, but not all, "X" cameras have another flash mode called "External Flash". This is designed for use with non-Fujifilm accessory flash units that will work in manual flash mode?

If your camera has this mode, then use it as I describe below. If it doesn't, then the following applies to "Commander" mode in your camera.

In this mode, we can even fit a wireless (radio) flash trigger to the camera, to drive the radio triggers.

Using this mode (or Commander on cameras like the X-T1), I've driven Yongnuo, Sony, Minolta, Canon *and* Fujifilm flashes *all at the same time*. Again, there will be much more on this in Chapter 4.

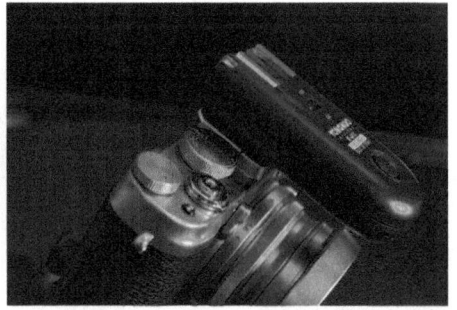

**Figure 3-6**: *More wireless flash. Though this time it was fired by a radio wireless trigger. This Yongnuo 603c unit (atop an X-platform camera) will happily trigger manual flashes (even at quite high shutter speeds for X100/S/T owners).*

All flash units fired via this "External" flash setting *only* work in manual flash mode – there is no TTL functionality. But don't let that put you off. It's not as difficult as it might sound, and if you learn how to use it, you'll find a plethora of great, cheap flash units to invigorate your lighting fun.

> **TIP:** *The interchangeable lens X-platform cameras have a maximum flash sync speed of 1/180$^{th}$ of a second – and many models have this exact shutter speed etched on the shutter speed dial to make it easy to use. Don't know what this means? No worries. Flash sync speed is discussed in Chapter 11.*

**Flash & Red-Eye Removal Tip:**  *Not that I recommend you perform red-eye reduction with flash, but some of the TTL flash modes can be used with Red-Eye Removal. Namely: auto, fill-flash (forced flash), slow sync, and rear-curtain (2$^{nd}$ Curtain) sync.*

*To select red-eye removal with your flash modes, turn* **Red Eye Removal → ON** *in the Menu. And since red-eye reduction is performed in some "X" cameras only when it detects a face, you might also need to enable Intelligent Face Detection (typically found in the menu under:* **Autofocus Setting → Face Detection → ON** *– or in the Q-Menu, of course).*

**Tip:** *The flash is always completely off in "Silent" Mode – which is intended to eliminate light and sound output from the camera for "quiet" shooting. Since flash is light, it is gone, along with a lot of other tiny things. You toggle Silent Mode via the "Silent Mode" Menu option.*

## X100/S/T THE LEAF SHUTTER & FLASH

You've probably gathered by now that I like the X100 series of cameras. If you're wondering why, it is mainly down to the features described in these next few pages. Put simply, the X100 cameras have a flash-related capability that very few other cameras (of any brand) offer:

### INBUILT 3-STOP ND FILTER

The X100 series has an inbuilt high-quality 3-Stop Neutral Density filter, switchable in the camera's menu or via a function button.

ND filters are frequently used to cut ambient light to allow slow shutter speeds – often to smooth out flowing water and give it a dreamy, graceful quality (see **Figure 3-7**). And you can use the inbuilt ND filter for just this purpose.

But in the X100 series, it serves another purpose: to cut ambient light to allow for high shutter speeds *and* wide open apertures. Giving you the ability to balance the ambient light of broad daylight with flash light, and all with a shallow Depth of Field! See **Figure 3-9**.

Enable the inbuilt ND filter (**ND Filter → On**) in the Menu, or program a function button by long-pressing it and selecting **ND Filter** from the options.

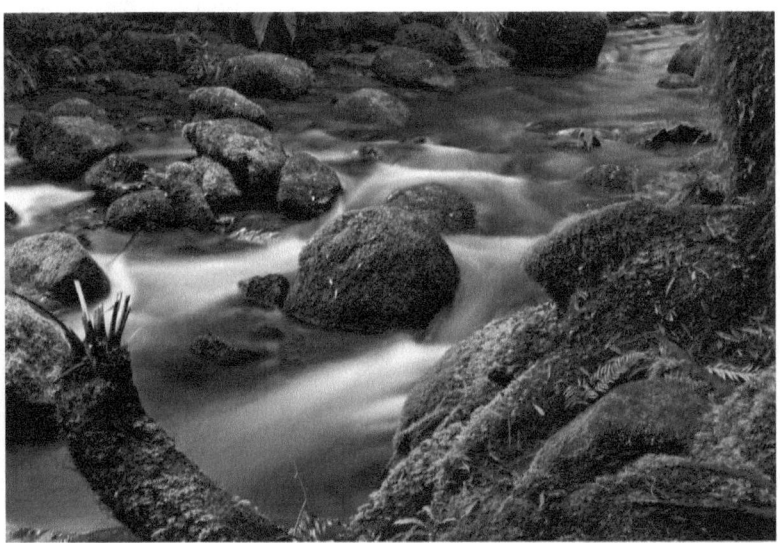

**Figure 3-7:** *A typical use for an ND filter – to create flowing, dreamy water. This shot from the mountain streams in Tasmania, Australia.*

## *LEAF SHUTTER*

What is it about a leaf shutter that makes it so appealing? *Why do photographers love them*, paying $3000-$6000 for a Schneider Kreuznach leaf-shutter lens that's no sharper, and apparently does the same job as a $1200 lens?

You may already know that leaf shutters have been a popular feature in photography since it's middle ages (think 1950's), though in truth, they existed way, way back in the 1890's. One reason you don't see leaf shutter lenses much now though, is their complexity. Which in turn, means, their high cost. If you're interested, this page by Riess has a great essay on the topic: http://www.kl-riess.dk/compur.eng.html. And a search for 'leaf shutter' on the internet will net you some interesting images to while away a minute or two.

So given the complexity and expense, why are leaf shutters still showing up in modern cameras? After all, the focal plane shutter (common to most cameras – and all interchangeable lens X-platform cameras) has stood the test of time. Well, for one, they are deadly silent – a pretty good feature for street and documentary photography. More importantly, they allow the camera to sync with flash at much higher shutter speeds than a focal plane shutter can, entirely changing our ability to compete with ambient light.

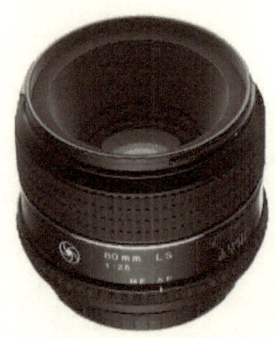

*Figure 3-8: A $3000 Schneider Kreuznach 80mm f2.8 AF Leaf Shutter lens.*

Let's examine how this works:

## REAL HIGH SHUTTER SPEED FLASH SYNC

Landscape photographers talk about the golden hour. The hour around dawn, or dusk when light takes on an almost magical quality. Paradoxically cameras are optimized for "normal" daylight, and yet images taken under those kinds of hard-light conditions seldom seem as wonderful as their counterparts shot in the golden hour (or under the influence of a photographer with a keen eye for light and the knowledge of how to achieve it from their equipment).

Until now, that is. The leaf shutter lens in an X100/S/T changes the photographer's ability to compete with ambient light. Add the in-built ND filter to the mix, and an external accessory flash or two, and you'll find yourself balancing flash with daylight to achieve the most wonderful light in outdoor situations. It's all about light *ratios* in relationship to ambient light.

The type of real high speed sync (RHSS) available with a leaf shutter lens is not at all like high speed sync (HSS) as you may know it. There are limitations placed on flash power delivered using HSS, brought about by the way the flash power is output (pulsed) during the period in which the shutter is open. These limitations not only *do not* apply with a leaf shutter and RHSS, you actually get *more* punch from your flash unit than you would if it were attached to a regular focal plane shutter camera.

This is a pretty big topic, and for X100/S/T owners I discuss it in much more detail in Chapter 11. In the meantime, feel free to dial up your shutter speed to $1/1000^{th}$ of a second, and head outdoors for some shooting.

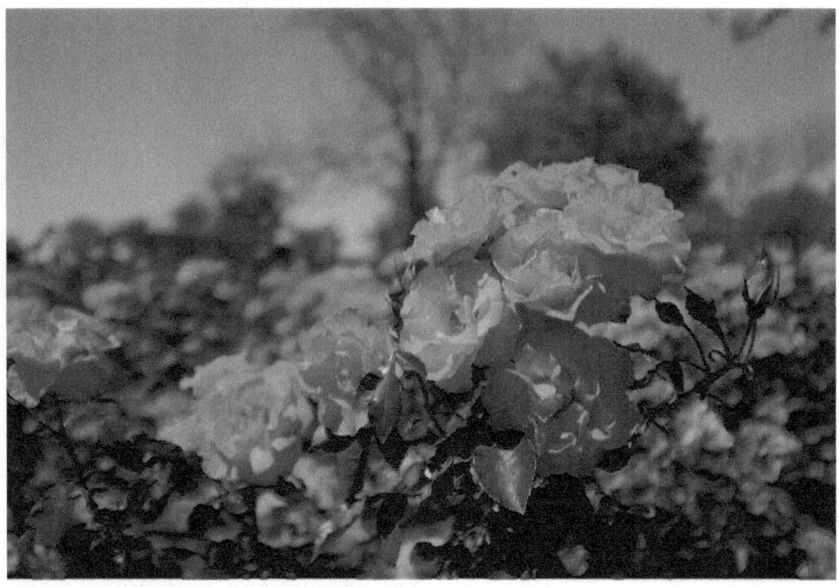

*Figure 3-9: Shot in the mid-afternoon sun on a warm, sunny summer day at $1/1000^{th}$ sec at F/2 using an off-camera EF-X20 flash (attached via a cord) to balance ambient light.*

Want shallow depth of field with that? Turn on the ND filter! **Figure 3-9** demonstrates how this all comes together. The high shutter speed ($1/1000^{th}$) cuts ambient light giving rich colours in the sky and trees. The ND filter means I could shoot wide open (f|2 in this case) so only the cluster of roses in the foreground is in focus. Add in the EF-X20 flash for some fill, and you produce a pleasing result in awkward lighting conditions.

COMING UP…

Look at any portrait studio and you'll see lights everywhere – though rarely on top of the camera itself. That's because professional photographers understand the *least flattering* place to put a flash is on the camera facing toward your subject. Where's the best place? *ANYWHERE ELSE!*

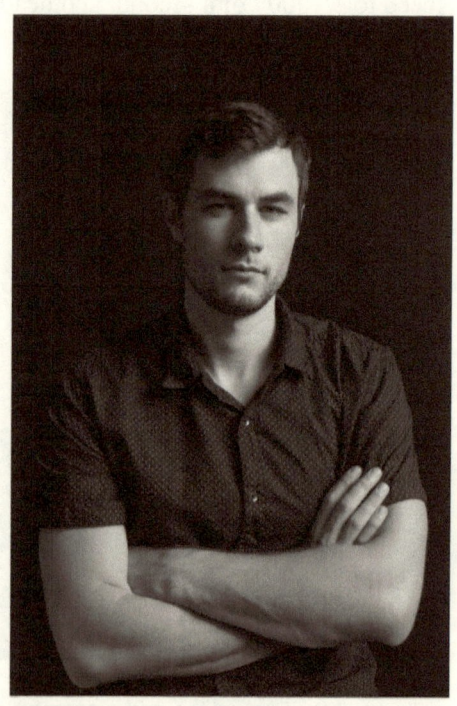

You can use cables to get your accessory flash away from your camera, and preserve automatic TTL flash exposure. Or you can go wireless, using Fujifilm's IR "Commander" Flash function – or go even further and use some wireless radio triggers.

Both the latter require you to manage flash exposure yourself (manual flash) – though this is not as daunting as it might seem, and it's well worth the effort for the huge benefits wireless flash can bring to your photography.

I cannot emphasize enough the significance of this feature. In fact, it is so important that I've devoted *several chapters* in the latter half of this book to

**Figure 3-10:** *Supercharge your creativity by getting your flash off the camera!*

mastering just this kind of flash photography.

For now, let's turn our attention to the flash models available to us when shooting with X-platform cameras.

# CHAPTER 4    FLASH MODELS

Before we go further, let's look at the available tools – the flash units you can trigger with your camera by hot-shoe, cable, infrared (wireless) or radio (wireless). While Fujifilm has a limited range of accessory flash models, if you're willing to go to manual flash, virtually any flash unit will work with your "X" camera!

## FUJIFILM ACCESSORY FLASH MODELS

Fujifilm flashes offer you something you can't do with third-party units. The camera knows about them, and can TTL meter for them (see Chapter 5 for more on this), in addition, two of the models offer manual exposure controls as well (see Chapter 8 for a discussion on manual flash metering).

Fujifilm have four flashes designed to work with the X-platform cameras. There are pros and cons for choosing one above the other which are outlined in the following table:

| Name | Notes |
|---|---|
| EF-42 | • Guide Number = 42. Most powerful of Fujifilm's accessory flashes<br>• Is large for the role, but works great on the camera's hot-shoe<br>• Can't trigger wireless flashes as "Master" *NOR* be an off-camera slave flash<br>• Does both TTL and manual exposure<br>• Flash head swivels and rotates for complex bounce<br>• Plastic case, LCD screen for controls<br>• Has an inbuilt IR light for focus assist in dark lighting |
| EF-X20 | • GN=20<br>• Works great on the camera's hot-shoe<br>• Can trigger wireless flashes as "Master"<br>• Can act as an off-camera wireless flash In "Slave" mode |

| | |
|---|---|
| 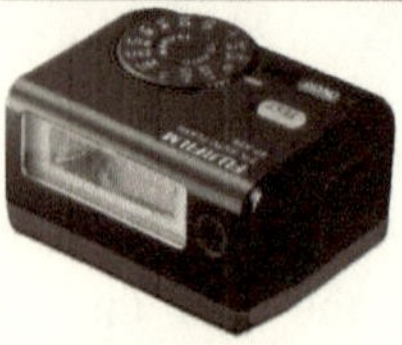 | • Does TTL and manual exposure<br>• Fixed, forward facing on hot-shoe.<br>• Mostly metal, robust, light weight, with external dials for EV and manual control |
| **EF-20** 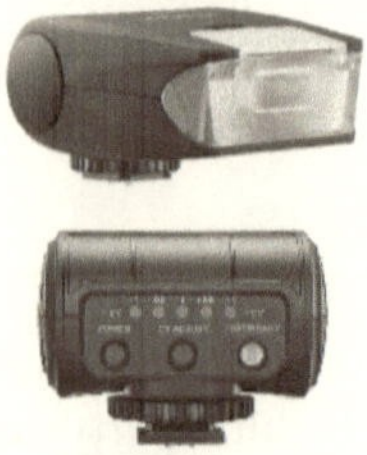 | • GN=20<br>• Works great on the camera's hot-shoe<br>• Can't be an off-camera wireless flash<br>• TTL only. No manual exposure<br>• Forward facing on hot-shoe. Head swivels up to 90° for top bounce<br>• Tiny and light. Plastic case. With buttons and LED controls 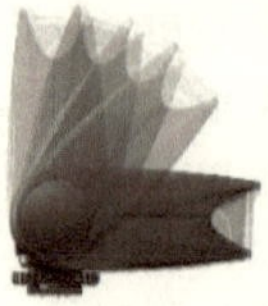 |
| **EF-X8** 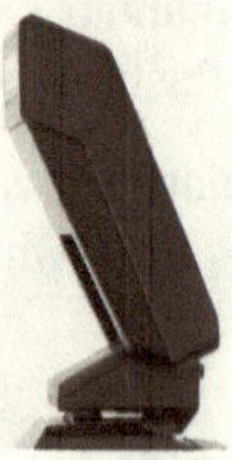 | • GN=8<br>• Currently only works with the X-T1<br>• Batteries not included – draws power from the camera<br>• Flips down for rapid flash-off 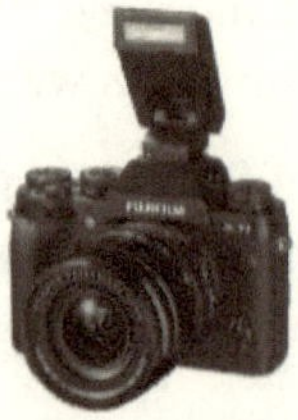 |

While I like the tiny EF-X8 flash included with the X-T1 for its pocketable size, my flash of choice among these is the EF-X20. You're probably thinking that's because it's retro, and suits the "X" cameras perfectly, but the real reason is the flash compensation dial, which makes it so easy to dial in adjustments. That, and the fact it can act as either a slave or master in the wireless flash system make this unit ideal. It's robust too with a mostly-metal case. The downsides are that it uses AAA batteries – which it seems to really like, and it is fixed. It doesn't flip or rotate for bouncing.

To get around the first issue, I use Sanyo

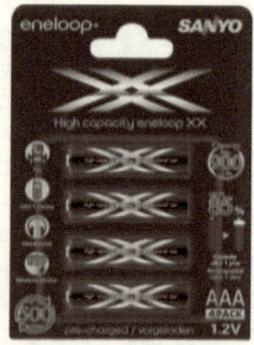

***Figure 4-1*** *High capacity batteries provide rapid recycle times.*

eneloop XX 950mAh HR-4UWXB batteries to get the fastest recycle times. A short TTL cable helps me around the second (see Chapter 7 for more).

To use this unit as a Master (and for normal use), slide the underside switch to "X". I'll explain the other two settings (and which to use, and when) further on.

---

**EF-X20 TIP:** *Rotate the mode dial atop the EF-X20 accessory flash from TTL Auto mode, to Manual flash mode, and it automatically instructs the camera of the change. You'll see the flash icon (top left in the viewfinder – and in the Q-Menu) change from "Forced Flash" (⚡), to this: ⚡. X100S owners will recognize this as "External Flash" (which really means "Manual Flash"). For other cameras (like the X-T1), searching the manual won't provide an explanation for this icon. But, just as it does with the X100, here it means "Manual Flash", and the icon is the same as the X100/S's "External Flash" icon.*

*In "X" cameras with programmed flash function buttons, you'll notice in this configuration, the flash button becomes inactive. Switch back to TTL on the flash unit though, and button functionality is restored.*

*Incidentally, since the EF-X8 does not have a manual flash setting, you will not see this icon with that unit. On some "X" cameras (like the X-T1), other third-party flashes and triggers show no viewfinder/LCD flash icon either – though there is still a Q-Menu icon indicating the correct flash mode.*

---

## THIRD PARTY FLASH MODELS

I stated earlier that virtually any third-party flash would work with X-platform cameras. And that's true. Though there are a few caveats.

Firstly, third party flash units will *NOT* work in automatic TTL metering mode (Through The Lens). Flash output must be manually controlled for all non-Fujifilm flash units, and therefore the flash itself must be capable of manual operation. (As of the time of writing though, there are good indications that this is going to change in the very near future. I have more on this a little further on.)

Next, the triggering voltage in some older flash units is much higher (often up to 400 volts) than for current models (6 volts or less), and this high voltage is applied across the contacts of the camera's hot shoe! In previous "X" camera manuals there was a warning (consider it dire) not to use such a flash unit directly on the camera. There are some great flash units like the Vivitar 283 and 285HV exactly like this. If you have these kinds of flashes, you *can* use them. There are a few units like the Wein Safe-Sync ($50), or Fotodiox SMDV Hot Shoe Safe Sync Adapter SM-512 ($15) that will render the flash safe to use. Mind you, if you're thinking of spending $50 on an adapter, there are some great third-party flash units for not too much more that might be worth considering. (I'll get to that shortly.)

High voltage is not a problem with modern flashes, but if you have any doubt at all, I suggest you research, or check with the manufacturer, or someone properly knowledgeable in your particular flash.

---

*Tip: Older flash units can often be had online for quite low prices. Those Vivitars I mentioned earlier are fondly remembered by many photographers, and quite a few of them are still in regular use. They have the ability to sync at quite high speeds (a bonus for X100/S/T users), and produce even, repeatable lighting.*

*If you have such a flash, or are looking to add some cheap units to your flash "tree", this website might help steer you as to the high-voltage safety issues so far as your camera is concerned:*
*http://www.botzilla.com/photo/strobeVolts.html .*

*Having said that, **you must check with a reputable source** before you attach any flash unit to your camera. I haven't researched any of that site's recommendations, and bear no responsibility for the accuracy of the information there. Just saying...*

---

I've had good success with various older flash units like Minolta 5600 flashes (which have a different mounting system to the "X" hot shoe). In manual mode, and with an appropriate cable or wireless trigger (radio wireless in my case) this unit works rather well.

If you have any relatively modern Nikon, Canon, Sony, or other brand flash built for a DSLR, that offers manual exposure, I'm reasonably confident you can use it with your "X" camera. Either directly atop the camera (though I'm going to suggest you *DON'T* do this later on in this book), or via a cable or wireless triggering system. Caveat emptor though. Check the triggering voltage if you are in any way unsure.

---

**Third Party TTL Flash:** *Earlier I mentioned third-party TTL flash. Probably by the time you read this, you'll be able to purchase this tiny 203g* 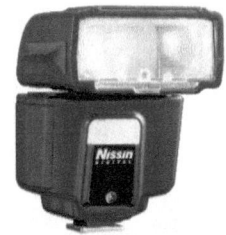 *Nissin i40, Fujifilm (X-platform) compatible TTL/Manual flash. This unit outputs GN40 @ 105mm, and GN27 @ 35mm, and offers both **manual and TTL operations** with your camera.*

*Don't read this to mean it offers wireless TTL capability. It doesn't. But atop an "X" camera (or on a cable), you have third-party swivel and tilt TTL flash.*

*Why is this unit noteworthy? These reasons stand out:*

*1) A third-party flash manufacturer is manufacturing a TTL flash compatible with Fujifilm's "X" platform flash system.*

*2) The unit provides manual flash control.*

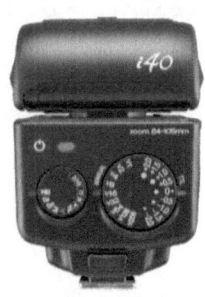

*3) TTL Flash compensation (±2 EV) is readily available on the flash body via a dial.*

*4) Modes are easily selectable via dial.*

*5) The flash operates with Fujifilm's wireless system, and with third-party wireless triggers. So it is good value as part of your lighting kit.*

*6) There's an LED video light built right into the front of the unit!*

*Visit this page for more:* http://www.nissindigital.com/i40.html

*Since it's not available at the time of writing, I'm not recommending this flash. But if it lives up to its promise, this could well be a unit worth having.*

---

If you are looking to acquire a new manual flash unit, I'm finding the Yongnuo 560 II or III models to be both cost effective and effective. Plus they play well with wireless triggers, *AND* they sync successfully at high enough speeds with leaf shutter cameras, giving great results when balancing ambient and flash light as discussed in this book.

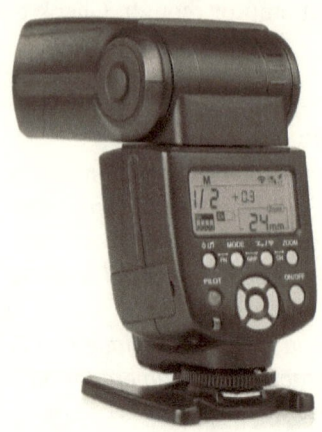

*Figure 4-2*   *A Yongnuo 560 III*
*manual only flash unit. The III has*
*the Yongnuo wireless receiver built*
*right in, whereas the II requires you*
*to attach a separate wireless*
*trigger.*

Here's a thing too: X-platform cameras can trigger these Yongnuo flashes in the same wireless (IR) way that they trigger Fujifilm flashes. I'll explain how this works shortly. Mind you, they still must be metered manually as there's no TTL metering for any non-Fujifilm flash units. But they do trigger - as will any third-party flash that has the ability to be triggered via infrared triggering, I suspect.

Recently, Yongnuo started shipping the very affordable YN560-TX – a remote manual controller, allowing you to set manual flash output for up to 6 groups of 560 III flash units right at your camera. Now that's pretty cool if you are working in a studio with multiple lights inside light modifiers. Read more on that in Chapter 7.

COMING UP…

Would it surprise you to know you can have a modern, high-powered (GN58) flash and wireless trigger that will work with your "X" camera, *and* an umbrella for around $100? If you really go overboard, another $30 will get you a lighting stand and hardware – and you'll have a portable lighting studio.

Having fun with lighting with your "X" camera is very affordable. Just look up Yongnuo 560 III and Yongnuo 603c II on the internet to see what I mean.

Up next we consider flash metering – then we're into the meaty stuff where we'll put flash to work for us.

# CHAPTER 5     FLASH EXPOSURE

Just as you must manage or compensate ambient light exposure via either manual exposure mode, or exposure compensation adjustments, the same is true when using flash.

This chapter examines flash exposure, concentrating on TTL flash and flash compensation.

## MANUAL FLASH

The concept of Manual flash is easy to understand. *You* set the light output from the flash by choosing a power output from full flash power (1/1) right down to 1/128 flash power. In fact, the lowest available power output varies with individual flash units. Most modern flashes support power outputs down to 1/128 of their full-power capabilities, but a flash like the venerable Minolta 5600 can only be set as low as 1/32.

Of course, what 1/2 flash means for one flash unit might be entirely different for the same 1/2 setting on another flash unit. As an example, consider what 1/2 means for a GN 20 flash (think EF-X20) compared to 1/2 power on a GN 58 or 42 flash. There is simply no easy way to equate power output between dissimilar units – and this is a big part of the confusion to be dealt with when first encountering manual flash exposure.

As you can expect, since this is how it works, your camera is obviously not aware of the amount of light a flash will deliver, so it actually does *nothing* to take this light into account (if you are shooting in Program, Shutter, or Aperture exposure modes). And in Manual exposure mode, you are completely on your own, with the camera expecting you to set ISO, shutter, aperture and flash power to create the desired result.

Since setting manual flash requires we cover off a few more things before jumping right in, I'm going to hold off on developing it further right here. But I promise you, I'll explain how to *accurately* set exposure for manual flash in Chapter 8 (don't worry, it's not hard). For now though, let's turn our attention to TTL flash.

## TTL METERING

Now seems like a good time to distinguish between TTL flash metering, and manual flash operation.

Through The Lens (TTL) metering of flash is automatic metering of flash light as you've come to expect from pocket cameras, and anything firing on "auto" mode to snap pictures.

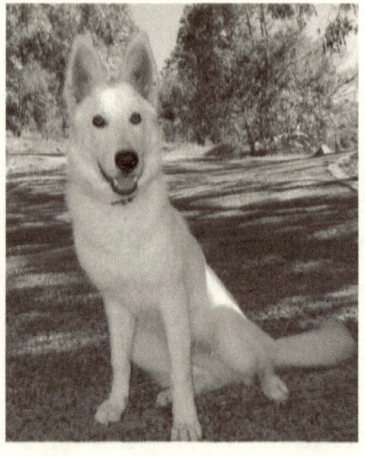

Fujifilm doesn't explain exactly how TTL flash metering is implemented in "X" cameras (there are a few ways it could be applied), so for the purposes of this discussion, let's think of it this way: since your camera knows (by metering through the lens) how much ambient light is being reflected back from your subject, it's able to calculate how much flash light is required to create a "proper" exposure given the current ISO, f/stop and shutter speed (even though it may be calculating these elements too, based on your camera settings). Once it knows this, it can instruct the flash on how much light to deliver when you take the picture.

*Figure 5-1* *TTL flash is your go-to everyday flash, and Fujifilm's implementation of it is excellent. Notice how it lifts the deep shadows in this image.*

Of course, given that the camera is trying to create a "normal" exposure, and yet often when you are using a flash, lighting isn't anywhere near normal, the result may not be quite what you are looking for. Oftentimes the result is white(ish) faces in a sea of darkness – though in my experience, "X" cameras do a pretty good job even in these difficult-to-expose-for situations.

You'll have noticed from the table in Chapter 4, that Fujifilm flash units all work in TTL metering mode when they are on the camera. Only the EF-X20 can be removed from the camera and used in IR wireless mode (Commander Flash Mode) *but* you lose TTL metering when you do this. Of course, three of the flash units can be attached to the camera via an accessory cable (not the EF-8), and still offer TTL flash operation, thereby allowing them to be removed some distance from the camera (we'll talk more about getting the flash off the camera shortly).

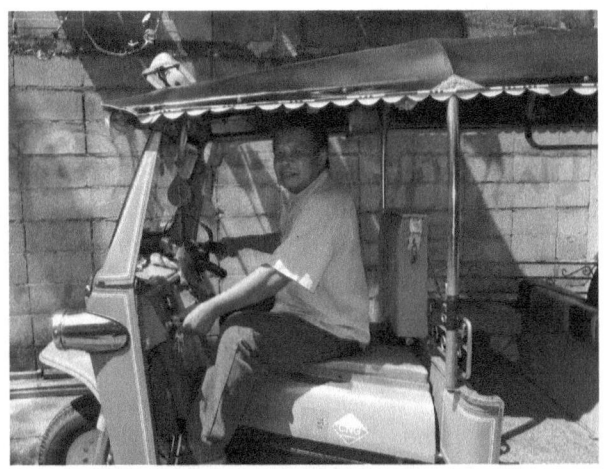

**Figure 2:** *Fill-flash used for daytime street photography to open up the shadows. Bangkok, Thailand.*

## FLASH COMPENSATION

Just as the camera has exposure compensation to adjust for ambient light exposures (in the P, A, S exposure modes), so too, flash has its own compensatory mechanism – called flash compensation no less!

My general rule of thumb for using flash compensation is to set my camera controls to expose for the background, and use flash to add light to the foreground (subject). In this application, the ability to wind flash compensation *down* can come in quite handy.

And similarly, as with exposure compensation and the semi-automatic exposure shooting modes (P, A, S), flash compensation only works in TTL (auto) flash modes – not in manual flash mode.

TTL flash is a great go-to, everyday flash application. It's easy, and quick, and doesn't require you to think much about the added light from the flash, and in X-platform cameras, the results will be acceptable much of the time. Combined with the camera's histogram and LCD, you can quickly tell if you need to adjust flash compensation up or down to improve the exposure. For this reason, I really enjoy the tiny EF-X20 flash with its mechanical flash compensation dial right on top of the unit. I'd like more than one stop either way though, but this is by far the best implementation of flash compensation currently available for any of the "X" cameras.

Apart from the meagre ±1 stop of flash compensation available on the EF-X20, flash compensation capability varies from camera to camera. Surprisingly, the X100/S only has ±2/3$^{rd}$ of a stop of flash compensation – but, (and it's a big but) it's buried 8 key presses (minimum) deep in the menu if you want to use it! On the other hand, the X-T1 has a more respectable ±2 stops of flash compensation in 1/3$^{rd}$ stop increments – a great boon, and one which I am very thankful for. But (and it's the same big but) it's buried *10 key presses* deep in the menu!

I've grumbled elsewhere (in other books) about how difficult it is to use this, but with the advent of reprogrammable Q-Menu options this seems set to change. (Flash compensation is one of the options you can program onto the Q-Menu on applicable cameras!)

Hopefully, Fujifilm will see fit to bring this Q-Menu advancement into current "X" cameras, and my grumbles will simply cease to exist. But for now, if you want quick access to flash compensation, the dial atop the EF-X20 flash unit is as good as it gets.

One thing that might surprise you, is that flash compensations are additive. Dial in flash compensation in the camera body, and flash compensation in a Fujifilm flash, and the effect is *cumulative*. So -2/3 in an X100S and -1 (stop) with an EF-X20 in the hotshoe, gives you a very workable -1 2/3 stop of flash compensation!

Of course, it's a bit unwieldy to use this way, and you must dive 8 key presses deep to set the camera straight again, but it does work!

I vary Flash Exposure Compensation values depending on what I'm shooting:

- If the flash is the main light source (90% or more) in a darkened room then I use ±0. This very likely won't give a great shot, but it will give you an image. If you know how to drag the shutter then you can switch to manual exposure and turn out some worthwhile results. Slow Synchro flash (Chapter 3) can serve you well here too.

- If I'm using an accessory flash or a white piece of paper to blend flash and ambient light, I often set this to -1/3rd (sometimes -2/3rd) so the result looks more "natural" and less like I used a flash. I might do the same if I'm bouncing light off a white ceiling or wall to augment ambient lighting.
- If I'm using the flash as fill flash on a sunny day to lighten shadows on faces and clothing as in Figure 5-3, I usually set flash compensation to -1/3rd or more – though in my estimation, the "X" cameras I have used have one of the best "fill flash" implementations in existence.
- For a completely different look, I put the leaf-shutter/flash combo to work in the X100 series, and set a high shutter speed – 1/1000th second with appropriate f/stop – to underexpose the background making it rich and colourful, and use the flash at anything down to -1 to light my foreground subject without having that stark flash look. Given that we're talking about the leaf shutter "X's" here, I can go further and turn on the inbuilt ND filter to cut ambient light further so I can shoot wide open (f/2 say) in this scenario, giving me a shallow depth of field in broad daylight! This will likely require setting FEC at ±0, or higher, or even adding one of the accessory flashes with more flash power (depending on your distance to the subject). Since this is one of the hugely unique (and fun) aspects of these cameras, this topic is covered in much more detail in Chapter 11.

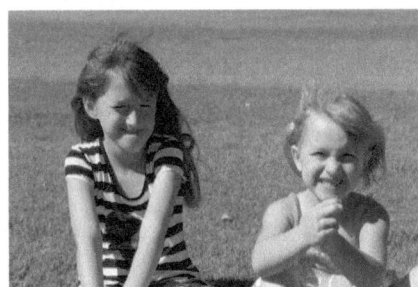 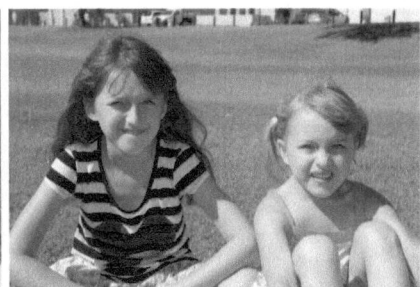

*Figure 5-3*: *A 95 degree day makes for harsh shadows. Not the best shooting situation by far. You can rescue it somewhat using fill flash. Dialing down your flash compensation can prevent that "flash" look if you need it. Left: Suppressed Flash (off). Right: Forced Flash (fill). I just didn't have the heart to keep my models out in the sun any longer.*

The flash compensation value (entered via the menu) is stored by the camera for future use, even if you turn the camera off. It won't survive a reset or firmware upgrade (though given the number of available opportunities, I haven't tested the latter). Without diving into the menu, there is no way of knowing what your flash compensation setting is, so if you adjust it, remember to put it back, otherwise you'll find yourself wondering what's gone wrong with your exposures.

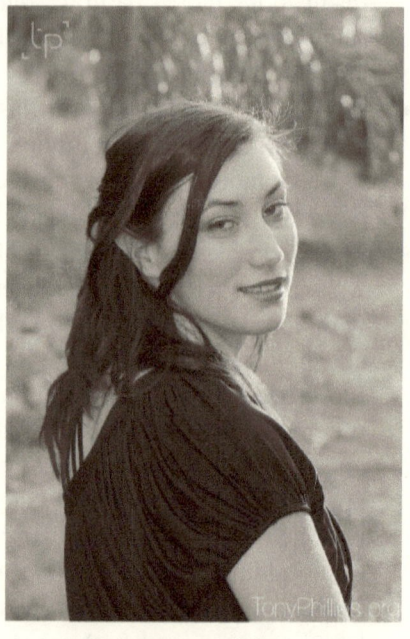

Finally, (and all my grumping aside) it's worth repeating that the X-platform of cameras have one of the best implementations of fill-flash I have encountered in a high-end camera, rendering flash images with better, less-flash like lighting than many DLSLs I've used or written about.

*Figure 4:* *Light is everything. Be on the lookout for light. Changing light can transform an average picture into something much more memorable.*

## COMING UP…

In the next chapter we look at how to get the best results using on-camera flash – including the use of home-made and commercial on-camera light modifiers.

# CHAPTER 6     ON-CAMERA FLASH

I'm sure you've heard this a hundred times, but one of the best things you can do to improve pictures taken with flash is to move the flash unit off the camera. Virtually anywhere other than where it sits on its hot shoe is a better place to be. Pictures taken with onboard flash can have red-eye, they look flat and possibly washed out (since the lighting is front-on), are frequently not exposed how you would like them to be, and often have dark backgrounds. Ironically though, this is how many people use an accessory flash.

Now I use onboard flash quite a bit too. Especially outside in the sunlight where it becomes fill-light rather than key light (which is usually the sun). And I have been known to keep my flash on the camera at a party or venue to make things easier to manage (depends whether I'm there "officially" or not too).

So, what if you're stuck with it, or are rushed, or not the "official" guy? I'm all for getting a picture vs no picture at all, even if it is overexposed (blurry, grainy etc). There are some quite recognizable images that are just like this (remember that picture of Albert Einstein with his tongue out?). Technically not great. But I really, really wish I'd taken it.

There are a few things you can do to make on-board flash work harder for you to overcome that "flash" look. So let's dig into these for a bit.

## BOUNCE FLASH

One of the worst applications of an accessory flash is to have it atop the camera, pointing directly at your subject in a darkish room (**Figure 6-1a**). And yet, one of the easiest ways to make it more palatable is to bounce its light off something. You've all seen people (probably someone saw you) with their flash pointing upwards to take advantage of a low, white ceiling (sometimes even if it isn't there! But that's another story – and not you. I didn't mean you...). Pointing the flash up, turns the ceiling into a large diffuser, and can give a much better effect (**Figure 6-1b**), wrapping light around your subject. You can also put light-coloured walls to similar use.

There's a third option. Many flash units come with a popup diffuser (some even have a white card) you can raise to reflect some light forward as fill light to reduce eye shadowing and the like, while the majority of the light goes through to the huge "diffuser" overhead (**Figure 6-1c**). I once saw a professional photographer shoot a whole wedding reception just this way.

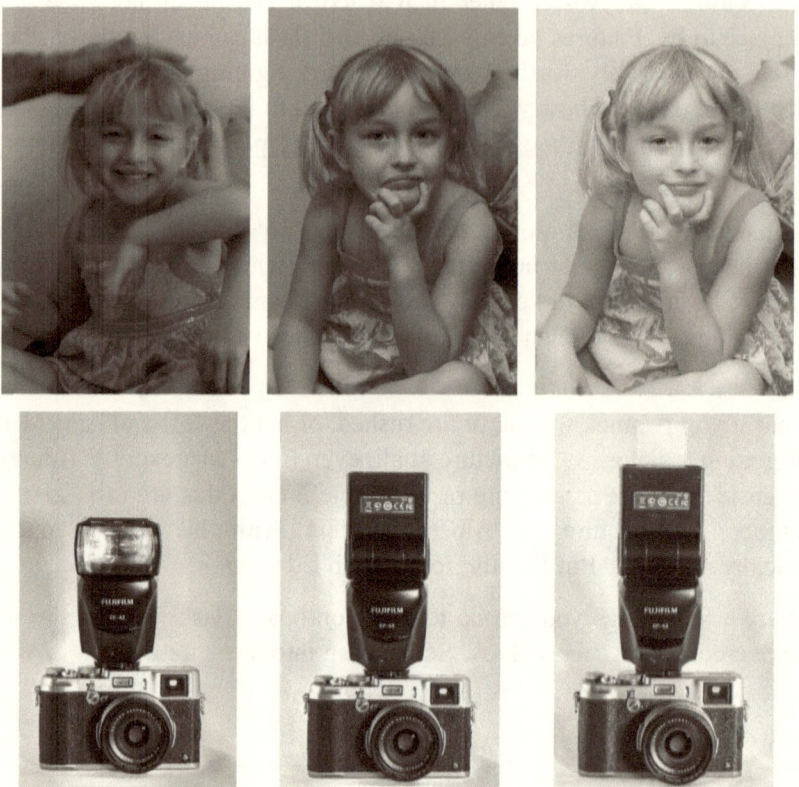

**Figure 6-1:**    *As you can see from this sequence of pictures, my cute young models soon got into the swing of things.*
**Left**: *On-camera flash. The resulting image is both typical, and not the best.*
**Centre**: *Bouncing flash off the ceiling softens light, wrapping it around the subject in a more pleasing way.*
**Right**: *For an even better result, raising the flash's inbuilt diffuser lifts shadows under eyebrows and chin by bouncing some light forward into the face. Note how transparent the inbuilt diffuser is. See tip 2 (next page) for more on this.*

## ON-CAMERA LIGHT MODIFIERS

There are other tricks you can employ to get even better results with on-camera flash. Add a modifier or two of your own! And what could be easier than the one pictured in **Figure 6-2a**. This is an on-flash diffuser on steroids! All we're doing here is pointing the flash up, and attaching a large piece of paper to the flash head with Velcro or a rubber band, thereby increasing the amount of light reflected forward onto our subject. It's easy, effective, inexpensive, and

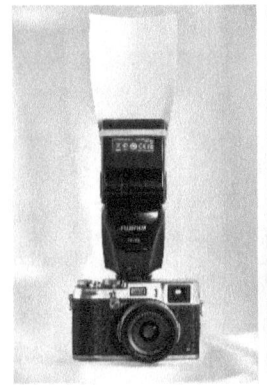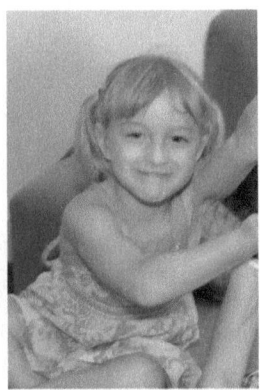

*Figure 6-2  The addition of a simple piece of white paper emulates natural light like no bare or bounced flash unit can. Quite a pleasing result!*

gives the most natural looking light you can get from an accessory flash.

*TIP 1*: Consider attaching a piece of paper to your accessory flash (pictured *Figure 6-2a*), even when shooting outdoors in sunlight with **no** ceiling to bounce off. (I know, I joked about this before). But the quality of fill light using this method is much better than bare flash alone – even though you obviously lose flash power by shooting light back into space.

*TIP 2*: While virtually every flash unit able to bounce light now has an inbuilt diffuser, I've found the paper still gives better results. Being a bigger diffuser, it produces softer light. And being solid white, it doesn't leak light back behind you when you use it like the inbuilt transparent diffusers do (see *Figure 6-1f*).

If you look on the internet, you'll see dozens and dozens (and dozens) of flash light-modifiers that do a job somewhat like my humble piece of paper. None of them are as cheap and easy to obtain or replace of course, but do they give better results?

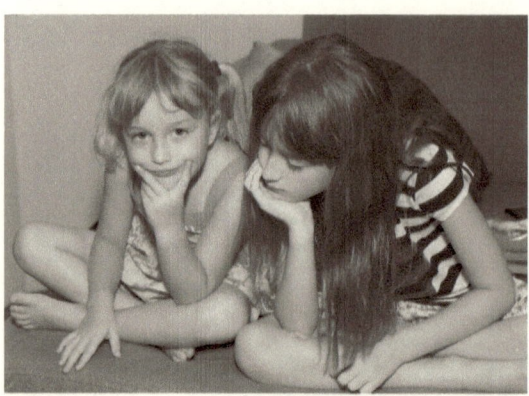

I've tried a few commercially built flash diffusers in my time, and one that gives decent results (I continue to use it), is the *Demb Saucer Flip-It* and added diffuser pictured in **Figure 6-3a**. In many ways this is *exactly* the same as my white piece of paper – though somewhat more handsome and professional looking (which can be a bonus in certain circumstances).

So why use it at all? Well, it can be adjusted to reflect more or less light forward onto the subject (there's a tilt mechanism). It can be used flat just like the paper, or concaved to give a dish, or saucer shape. This is its biggest advantage, since it emulates a white ceiling even where there isn't one! It works easily in both horizontal and vertical camera positions (though you need the EF-

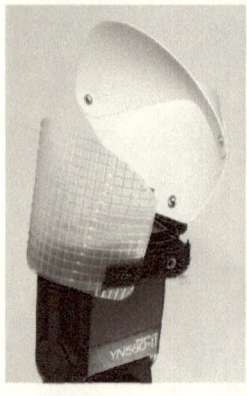 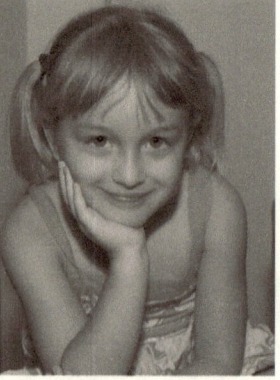

*Figure 6-3    Bottom Left: The Demb Saucer flip-it adjusts to push more, or less light forward onto your subject. The saucer emulates a ceiling even where there isn't one. In these two images our subject(s) are lit differently with the flip-it.*
*Top: The flip-it adjusted to push more light forward – giving a little more specularity. Bottom Right: And tilted back a bit for a little less direct light.*

42 to make the most of this), and if you use the additional front diffuser

(also pictured), light going straight forward from the flash is further softened.

Is it worth it? You be the judge. Compare the results of this commercial diffuser (**Figure 6-3b**) with those from my paper diffuser in **Figure 6-2b**.

I'm not trying to sell this product, but if you're interested, visit dembflashproducts.com.

There are many other kinds of light modifiers that give even better results than these if you're willing and able to put the flash anywhere else other than on the camera (see Chapter 10 for more on these modifiers). Now it's time have some fun and move past any last vestiges of separation anxiety and get our flash out there.

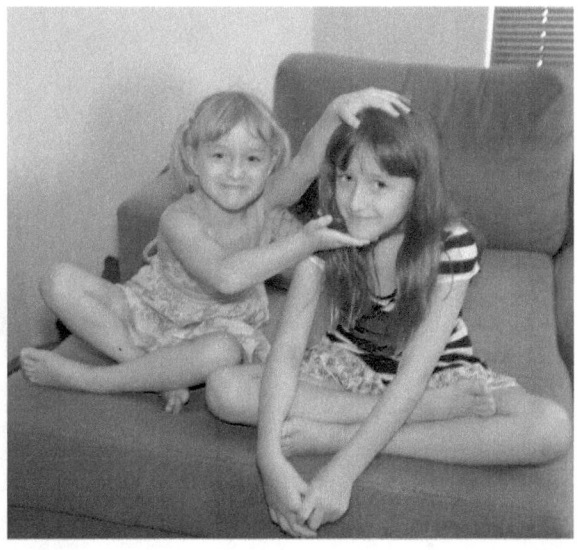

*Figure 6-4* The full example (from *Figure 6-2*) of the kind of natural light you get using a simple piece of white paper.

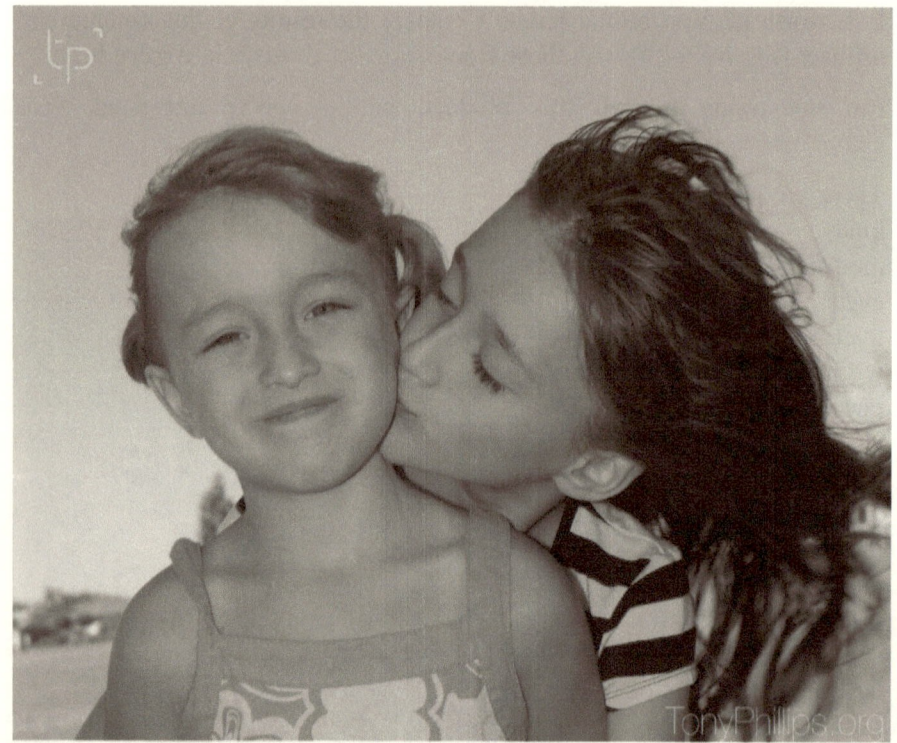

**Figure 6-5** *An open-shade EF-X20 flash portrait. 1/70th second. A nice **on-camera** flash image from an X100S.*

## COMING UP...

Now let's turn our attention to the plethora of ways you can get flash *off* the camera and get really creative.

# CHAPTER 7　　　　OFF-CAMERA FLASH

Getting the flash off the camera is all about modelling light. This gives you so much more control over *where* light comes from, and *what* is in shadow, than onboard flash ever can. By doing this, you can add drama to your images. **Figure 7-1** shows a family portrait using off-camera flash with a softbox diffuser.

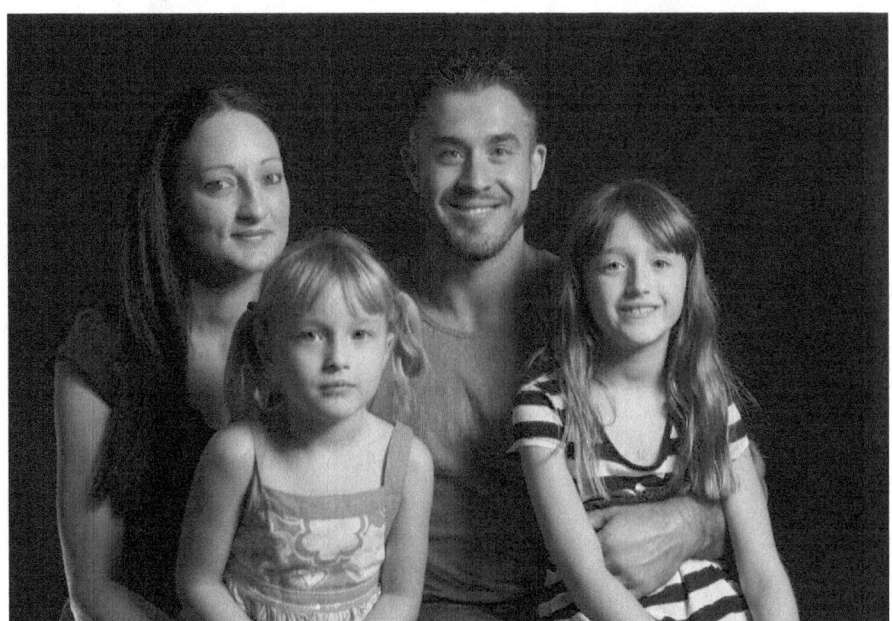

*Figure 7-1*: *Move the flash off-camera for high impact images people will treasure. A fun family to work with.*

Many people are nervous about using off-camera (wireless) flash, but they shouldn't be. It's not all that difficult, and the results speak entirely for themselves.

So before we dive into this fascinating topic, let me whet your appetite more by showing you examples of what you can achieve just by adding a little bit more to your daily photography grab-bag.

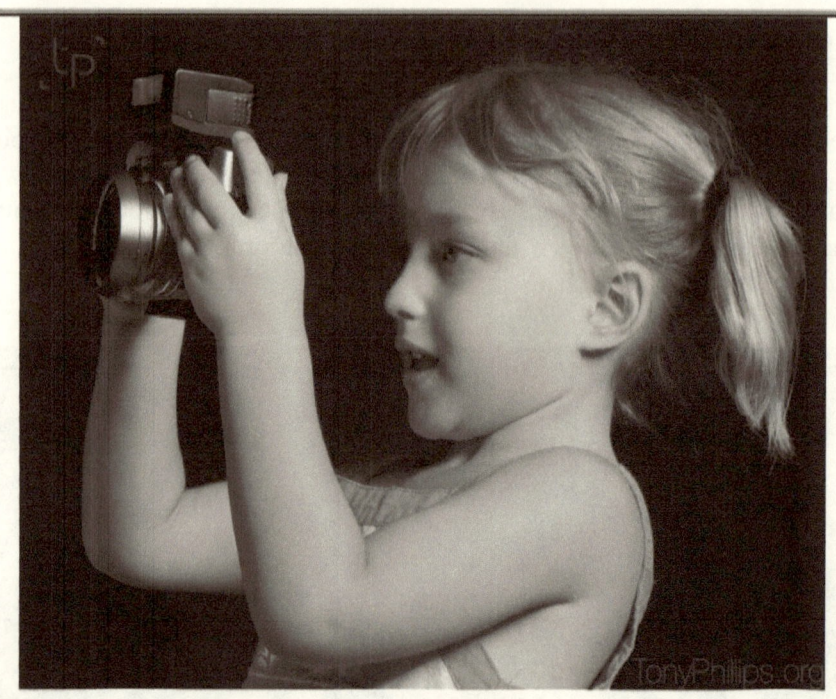

*It turns out I **will** lend my camera if the right gal comes along... ☺    Mariah was captivated by the X100S, giving me time for both a wide and a close-up. A two flash scenario. Softbox to the right as key-light. Tiny rim-light behind and left of image.*

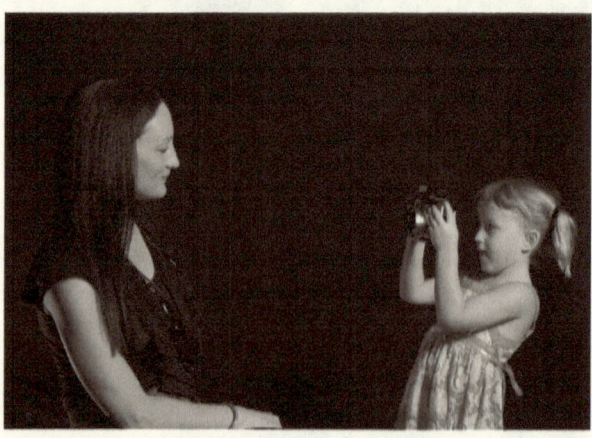

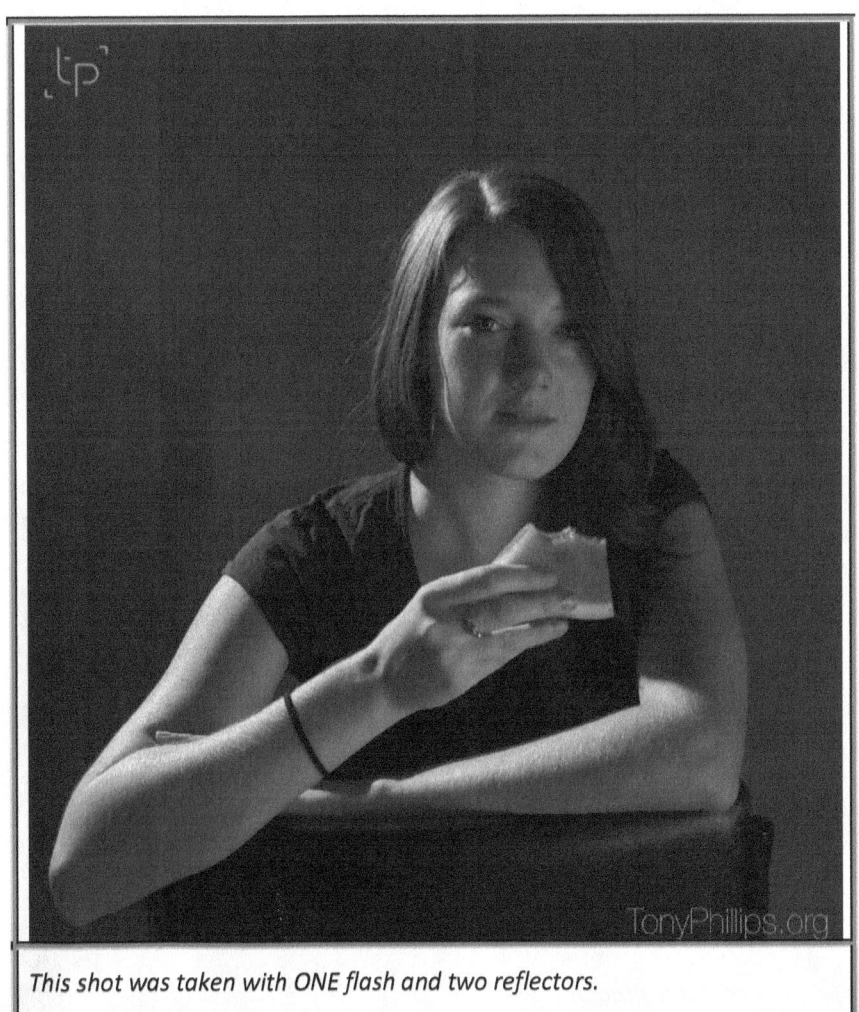

*This shot was taken with ONE flash and two reflectors.*

The above shot uses *ONE* flash, and shows off the benefits of getting your flash off the camera. In this case, the flash was *BEHIND* the model and over her right shoulder. When the flash fired, the light traveled over the model's shoulder (brushing her hair), and onto a large reflector in front, and to her left. It then bounces onto the left side of her face, *AND* to a second reflector on her right side – which in turn bounces a small amount of light onto the right side of her face. Recall, I called this "modelling light" earlier.

*The one-light setup for the previous image.*

*This demonstrates the versatility of off-camera flash and some reflective ingenuity.*

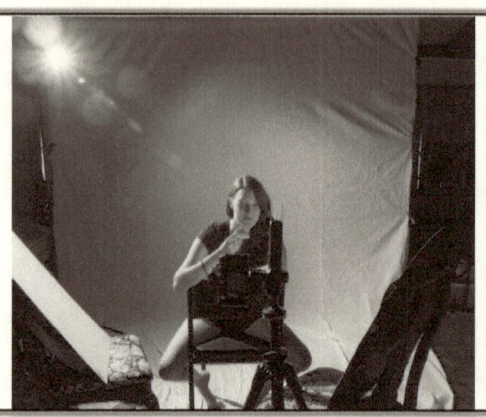

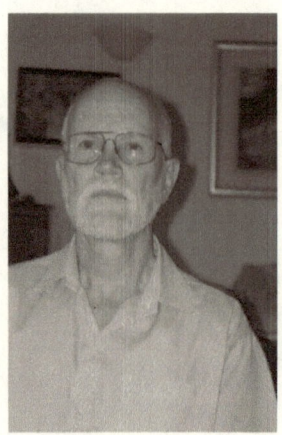

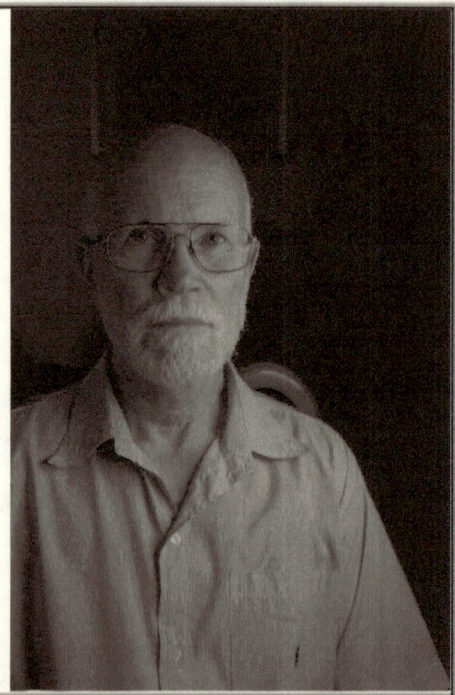

*Go from boring to dramatic in the same setting just by controlling your light!*

*This shot uses one flash, a softbox, and a reflector to add a hint of light on the right side of the face for added definition.*

So what's the best way to separate your camera and flash? At the start of this section, I called it "wireless". But you *can* do this easily using cables – which allows you to retain TTL automatic flash metering using Fujifilm flashes.

Apart from this though, *all* other off-camera flash options (including Fujifilm) require you to manually control flash output for proper exposure. I'm going to cover that before we leave this chapter, but just for the time being, let's consider what off-camera flash options we have at our disposal.

## FLY BY WIRE - CABLES

Using cables to connect your Fujifilm accessory flash to your camera is the closest thing to having it *on* the camera (you retain automatic flash metering), and yet you gain some of the benefits of off-camera flash.

The obvious drawback with wires is, well, the wires themselves. They are easy to trip over, and there are physical contacts to be concerned with, *and* they have limited operational range.

So what's the upside? As mentioned previously, attaching any of the Fujifilm accessory flash units this way allows you to retain TTL (auto flash) metering. Which means your camera will do its best to meter for added flash light without you manually managing flash exposure! And like some of the examples shown earlier, you can achieve quite pleasing results this way.

I can tell you too, if you're shooting

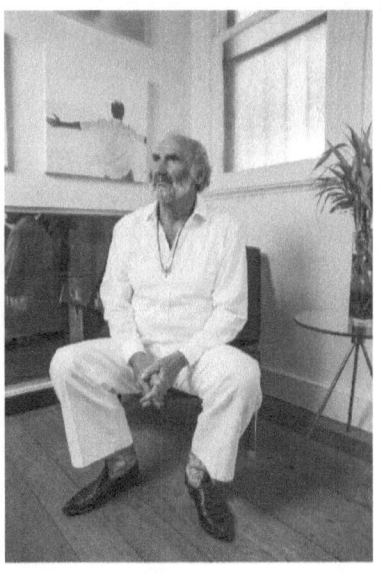

*Figure 7-2:* Dr. Jerzy Dyczynski can hardly sit still. He was relaxing back in the chair chatting, while I photographed. Then suddenly sat up and forward, altering my manual flash exposure dramatically. Luckily I was shooting RAW. The pose lasted three seconds!

subjects that don't sit still, TTL metering can save the day. And I don't mean babies and kids either. I recently did a job with a prominent Perth scientist and Dr. who quite simply wouldn't sit still. If you're experienced at manual flash metering, you'll know that moving lights even a few feet, impacts quite a bit on exposure. If your subject suddenly lurches forward three of four feet (a meter or so) into what you consider a good pose, but you're shooting manual flash, you had better be shooting in RAW too (where you have some grace to reel in exposure), or you *will* lose the shot. TTL might save you here. So if you're a manual flash aficionado, don't discount auto TTL mode. It has its uses.

If you buy straight TTL cables (not the curly types which act as springs to tug your light stands over at the slightest provocation), you can move lights quite some distance from your camera. Clearly, this is most suited to a studio, or other controllable environments.

> **X100/S/T Tip:**   *TTL metering is not the only benefit associated with using cables if you're shooting with a leaf shutter camera. Probably the biggest benefit relates to a unique feature of the X100 series of cameras which I discuss in Chapter 11 – Real High Speed flash sync. In brief, all radio wireless triggering mechanisms eat up tiny amounts of time in the transmission of the radio signal. Cables don't have this problem. Communication is virtually instantaneous, which means you can sync at much higher shutter speeds when using cables vs radio wireless triggers.*
>
> *Of course, outdoors, in sunlight is the situation where you are most likely to be using high shutter speeds (to control ambient light), and where cables are also the most difficult to manage.*

Given the difficulties using cables outdoors, I don't tend to use them much, unless…

I'm handholding the flash, or have it somewhere quite near the camera. In this situation, I have a 1.8mt (curly!) cable which allows me to retain TTL metering for the tiny EF-X20, *and* have the flash off-camera – though not too far away (see **Figure 7-3**). This is how I bounce flash with the EF-X20! (Incidentally, curly cables are ridiculously never anywhere near as "long" as their measurements make them out to be. Mine is good for nearly a metre (3 ft). After that, whoever is holding it is tugging on the camera!)

As with mounting third-party flash units directly on any X-platform camera, attaching them via cable does *not* give you TTL metering either. You're still on your own as far as managing flash exposure. Now this is not as problematic as it might seem. But if you're going to use these kinds of flashes, perhaps some of the following off-camera triggering options might suit you better.

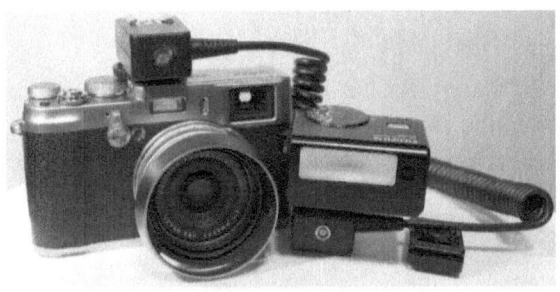

**Figure 7-3:** *By attaching a short TTL cable, you can point your Fujifilm flash anywhere for creative flash bouncing, retaining easy auto TTL flash metering to boot!*

One of the upsides to using cables is that it doesn't require line of sight between your camera and the remote flash unit. This is not the case with the next off-camera flash option on our list.

---

*Tip:* *If you want to use high shutter speeds with flash (for X100 series cameras)* ***and/or*** *use your "X" camera's TTL metering (almost) irrespective of where you place your flash, you can obtain straight, non-curly cables of various lengths. Straight cables* ***are*** *actually as long as advertised (You can get cables up to 10mt in length!). You can anchor them to the legs of stands and tripods, minimizing tripping hazards. Here are some suppliers you might be interested in:*

*ocfgear.com*         *flashzebra.com*         *michaelbass.blogspot.com.au*

*If you're handy with a soldering iron, another option is to purchase a canon compatible TTL curly cable and some CAT 5 cabling, and make your own.*

## IR WIRELESS

Infrared Wireless flash triggering as implemented in X-platform cameras is about as simple, yet effective as it gets. Set to the correct modes, the camera's inbuilt flash (or an EF-8 on an X-T1), or the EF-X20 on the camera, will emit a burst of light instructing the "slave flash(es) to fire.

It's best if the "master" and "slave" flashes are in direct line of sight, though the triggering pulse from the camera is sufficiently strong enough to communicate with a flash by reflecting off a wall, ceiling, or indeed the subject itself.

Apart from the absence of wires, one of the benefits of IR wireless flash is the freedom to place "slave" flashes just about anywhere they can "see" the triggering pulse. And not just one slave. You can use as many as you want to light the scene to your liking.

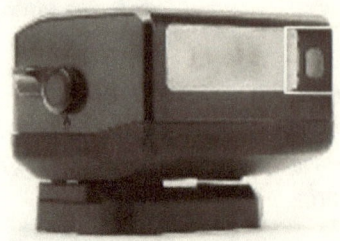

There's a notable downside to using IR wireless to trigger flashes though; outdoors it's not as reliable as using it in a studio or indoors. There are two reasons for this. Bright sunlight can interfere with triggering, and line of sight becomes even more significant – partly because there are less objects to bounce the triggering signal off.

*Figure 7-4: The infrared sensor at the front of your slave flash (yellow squares) must be able to "see" the incoming triggering pulse from the master. Line of sight works best, but it's sensitive enough to pick up the signal from light bouncing off walls or other objects.*

But there's a worthwhile upside too. *IR is fast*. There's no lag in the signal, no conversation between flash units (so it's as good as cable for high speed X100/S/T shutter work). And you can easily drive multiple flash units to boot. Of course, using this outdoors with a leaf shutter camera to balance ambient sunlight with flash tends to push the triggering system into an environment in which it is least reliable, but most desirable. But if it's working though, it does work well.

There are two implementations of infrared wireless flash triggering you can use with the all X-platform cameras:

*FUJIFILM WIRELESS FLASH – "COMMANDER"*

The first of these is the Fujifilm "Commander" wireless IR flash system. At the time of writing, there is only one Fujifilm accessory flash (EF-X20) that can operate this system as either master or slave flash – though I would expect this to change in time.

As mentioned earlier, there's no TTL metering with these flashes, and you can't rotate the IR sensor on the flash unit like you can with third party kit to align it for best line of sight to your camera. So with the baby EF-X20, you are essentially relying on reflected signal to provide triggering for you. This makes using it outdoors somewhat problematic.

Commander flash requires a minimum of two flash units – though the inbuilt (or EF-8) flash will happily work as the "Master" in this situation. You can have as many EF-X20 slave flashes as you want, and these can be placed anywhere in the room as long as they have a way to receive the triggering signal coming from the Master – either by direct line of sight, or after it bounces off a wall, ceiling or something you placed especially for the purpose. (It's pretty resilient indoors. I found with the camera and flash back to back it still fired successfully in a large room!).

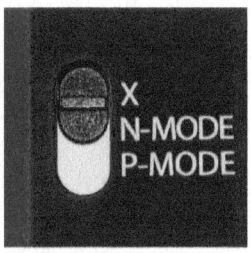

*Figure 7-5: Select N-MODE on the EF-X20 flash selector for Slave operation, and "X", to use it as Commander "Master" flash.*

The rest is simple. Just follow these few steps:

1. First, we must put the EF-X20 Slave flash into wireless mode. Do this by moving the selector on the underside of the flash to "N-MODE". This tells it that there will be no pre-flash, and it should fire when it receives the Master signal. Unless something changes, you will not use "P-MODE" with any "X" camera. P-MODE is expecting a pre-flash, and X-platform cameras do not do that.
2. Next turn the exposure dial on the flash to one of the white manual settings (we'll talk about how to accurately set exposure shortly).

Remember the red settings are for TTL auto flash, and that doesn't work in wireless Commander mode.

3.  If you are also using an EF-X20 on the camera as Master, the flash selector (switch) must be set to "X" for Commander/flash firing. Turn the flash mode dial to TTL Auto (for Commander 🔲 control). Putting it in manual flash mode will let the camera think it's just driving the flash in manual flash mode, and the onscreen flash icon looks like this: 🔲 (which we discussed earlier – page 37). Of course, you can still take the shot in manual flash mode, and the resulting flash pulse *will* trigger the remote flashes anyway. Though be aware, if you use full power in manual mode, it will deliver a full burst of light that exceeds the triggering pulse by quite a bit.

4.  Now set the camera's flash mode to "Commander" 🔲. You can do this through the Q-Menu, though with some cameras (see **Figure 7-6**), pressing the flash function button a number of times achieves the same result.

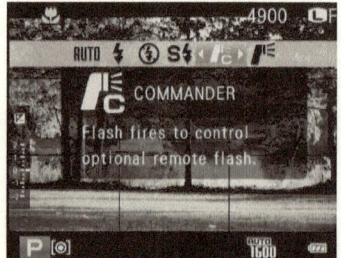

5.  Now place slave flash(es) anywhere in the room, ensuring they receive the Commander signals from the camera. There's no way to test this other than by firing off a shot.

*Figure 7-6:* An X100S screen shot. Select "Commander" to control EF-X20 Fujifilm accessory flashes wirelessly.

6.  Next you must set the manual flash exposure for each flash unit. For the moment, I'll assume this is done (there's a whole section on this in Chapter 8).

7.  Shoot away!

8.  Once you're finished with your photo session, you may want to put the slave EF-X20 back into "X" flash mode, and return the camera's flash setting to "Forced Flash" (fill flash) so it all works as you expect the next time you grab your camera.

With this setup, you can have one or many slave flashes in the room – and when you take the picture they will all fire with whatever manual intensity you set each one to have.

That's it! Experiment with placement of your strobes to create the mood you're looking for. Use them to highlight someone's hair, create a silhouette, add drama with ratio lighting (yet to come), bounce light from interesting angles. In short, to add drama and mood to your pictures just by moving the lights around!

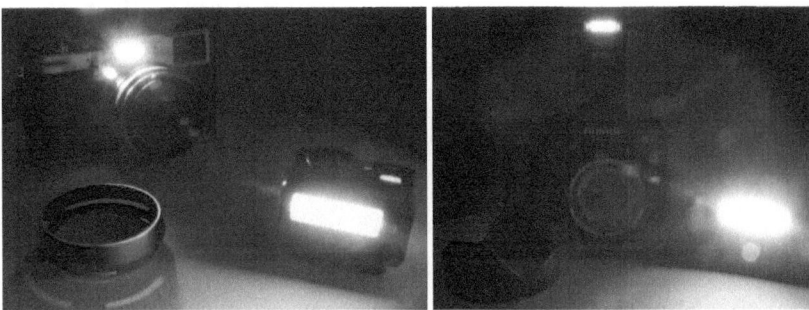

*Figure 7-7:* Look Ma! No wires! **Left**: With no remote in this X100S, I needed the timer for this one. **Right**: I used WiFi and a phone to trigger the shutter.

*Tip:* Not all flash functions work exactly the same across all X-platform cameras. To illustrate this, here's a tip from my X100S book:

"Turn the EF-X20 on in "X" (master mode), and plug it into the hot shoe, and the camera will automatically switch to Commander mode – irrespective of the current flash setting."

And now the same tip from my X-T1 book:

"Turn the EF-X20 on in "X" (master mode), and plug it into the hot shoe in TTL mode, and the camera will take control of the flash according to the current flash mode you have selected via the Q-Menu.

Dial in manual flash – either before or after mounting though, and the camera recognizes you are in manual flash mode and shows you the secret "I know we're in manual mode!" icon - $I^E$."

I expect the latter functionality to become standard across new "X" cameras – and perhaps become retrospective with firmware upgrades for existing models.

## THIRD PARTY IR WIRELESS

Here's a really cool thing. There are quite a number of other third-party flash units that can be used almost exactly as described above. The Yongnuo 560 (II or III) I mentioned earlier in this chapter has an optical triggering mode, and can be triggered by either the EF-X20 or inbuilt (EF-X8 for the X-T1) flashes. The diminutive Nissin i40 does exactly the same.

There's no real drawback to using third-party flashes, since you must already manually meter to use IR wireless flash anyway.

Using these types of optically triggered flash units is simple. Here's an example using the Yongnuo 560 II:

1.  First, put the Slave flash into optical wireless mode. Do this by turning the unit on, and pressing the MODE button a few times till you highlight "S1" (slave 1) as the flash mode (**Figure 7-8**). This is equivalent to N-Mode on the EF-X20.

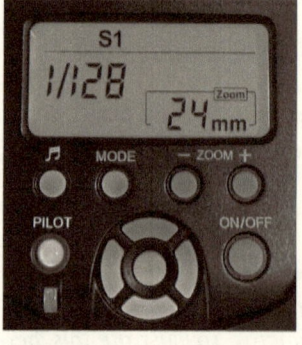

2.  If you are also using an EF-X20 on the camera as Master, its Wireless Slave flash selector (switch) must be set to "X" for Commander/flash firing.

3.  As before, set the camera's flash mode to "Commander" via the Q-Menu or flash button (if applicable).

*Figure 7-8:   Getting the Yongnuo 560 II to work with your "X" camera is as easy as selecting "S1" as the flash mode.*

4.  Again, place slave flash(es) anywhere in the room, ensuring they receive the triggering signals from the camera.

5.  Next, press the left or right arrow buttons on the 560's flash controller to manually adjust flash power output (**Figure 7-8**) for flash exposure. We'll talk about how to get the exposure right in the section on Manual Flash Exposure a few pages on.

6.  You're ready to shoot!

7.  Once you're done, return the camera's flash setting to "Forced Flash" so it all works as expected the next time you grab your camera.

That's all there is to it! You can use as many flashes as you like in this arrangement, and any unit that will do basic optical triggering will probably work.

## *INTERMIXING FUJIFILM AND THIRD PARTY IR WIRELESS*

We're not quite done with infrared flash just yet. It turns out you can seamlessly mix Fujifilm EF-X20 and third-party wireless flashes to light your composition. Just follow the steps in the previous section, treating your X20 as one of the boys. Remember to use N-MODE on the X20 – which is equivalent to S1 on the Yongnuo. Other branded optically triggered flashes will have a similar, simple setup.

One thing to keep in mind: if you're shooting in a crowd of photographers, optical triggering will be an issue, as the slave flashes *will fire* when they "see" *any other flash*, thinking it's their triggering signal. There's nothing you can do to overcome this since this is the simplest of triggering systems, and there is no "channel" selection as there are with radio wireless triggers.

## *WILL THE CONTROL BURSTS AFFECT EXPOSURE?*

You bet it will. (See **Figure 7-9**) In fact, to trigger external flashes, "Commander" mode outputs a constant-power burst of light without regard to metering, so it's going to be more noticeable on close subjects.

Out of curiosity, I did some informal testing with various X-platform cameras, putting them in manual exposure mode and using an external exposure meter in a simple low ambient-light flash test to see what the difference was in output between TTL and Commander.

Some "X" cameras output a full stop of light more than the equivalent TTL pulse the camera chose to light the scene. Others output *3 full stops of light* more in the same test!

I repeated the test, varying camera distance to the meter, and found that as flash-to-subject distance widens, the impact of the "Commander" pulse is less obvious. At 6 feet, for instance, the reading is virtually the same between the two outputs. While this kind of testing is in no way comprehensive, it is obvious that the closer the subject is to the camera, the more the Commander flash burst contributes to exposure. And at three feet, it quite adversely alters exposure!

At two metres, the reading was virtually the same between the two flash outputs. While this kind of testing is in no way comprehensive, it soon became obvious that the closer the subject was to the camera, the more the Commander flash burst contributed to light exposure. And at three feet, it was *stops* of light!

What is happening here is "Commander" emits a fixed power burst to trigger external flashes, and Forced Flash is TTL metering (despite shooting in manual exposure mode) to give a "proper" exposure. Combine this with what you know about light falloff, and you can see why the ratio between the two does not seem so apparent.

The takeaway is, the trigger pulse can have an undesirable impact on your exposure. And there are circumstances where you're not going to be happy with this at all.

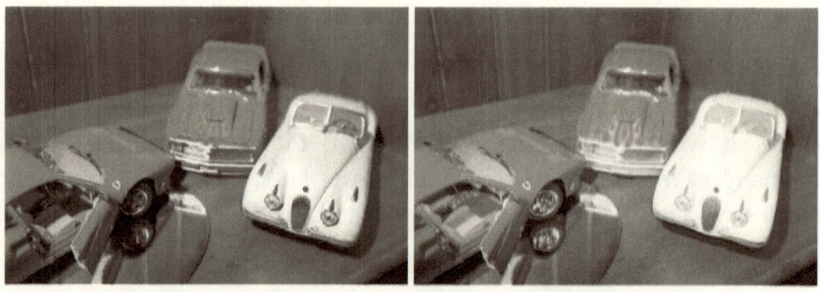

**Figure 7-9:** *Unless you do something to attenuate it, light from the Master flash "FIRE!" command can unduly influence your exposure – especially for close subjects. For these test shots a wireless flash was placed high on the left.* **Left:** *Film taped over the onboard flash per* **Figure 7-11** *blocks unwanted light from the "FIRE!" command.* **Right:** *Added light from the onboard flash's "FIRE!" command.  It's even more noticeable on a large screen. These models are approx. 12" (30cm) in length.*

So what can you do to remove "Commander" lighting from the equation? After all, it is on-camera flash we we're trying to avoid by using Commander mode at all, right?

Actually, let me start with one thing that doesn't work. No matter how much you dial down flash compensation, you cannot remove the onboard Master flash from the exposure equation.

Now onto some ideas that do work. If you've been reading up on this, you would have come across many options like these:

Tape an IR gel over the camera's flash to cut out visible light. This must be an *IR pass* gel to work, not on *IR cut gel*. Lee Filters have such a product (#87) that should work.

Tape a piece of E6 slide film (developed without exposing) over the flash, to do the same thing. This is cheaper, and equally effective. You could even buy a whole roll, and hand it right back over the counter to be developed. Ask them not to mount it in slide holders, and not to cut it. You just want the developed roll back to store with your other goodies.

You could, of course, use a commercially available screw on IR (infrared lens filter). About 850-900Nm should do the trick, and a suitably small one can be had quite cheaply from internet vendors since it doesn't require optical perfection. If you're into IR photography, recall that the 720Nm filters everyone loves, actually allows the red-end of the visible light spectrum through, so you don't want to use these. Mounting the filter on your camera flash is a bit of a bugbear too, but so I could be sure, I had to test it – and it works effectively!

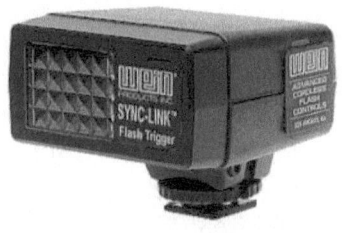

Another suggestion from Shawn Brenneman on twitter is: "stacking any deep red gel with a deep blue one (say Rosco #27 with #85). It'll look black, but IR will transmit." Clever – and small sample packs of gels are inexpensive.

*Figure 7-10*: *The Wein Sync-Link is an IR only wireless trigger that will fire optical flashes without adding light to the exposure from atop the camera.*

Here's another more serious suggestion: Use an IR only flash trigger instead of your camera's flash or the EF-X20 to fire an Infrared only triggering pulse. The Wein Sync-Link will do the job at around $70 (cheaper than buying a second EF-X20 by a good way). But there are even cheaper units on the market that do the same thing. These IR triggers look, sound, and act (and have a charging cycle) quite like a small flash except they only emit infrared light, so they don't influence your exposure, yet the remote flash(es) "see" the triggering signal just the same.

If you're using an EF-X20 as Master, you could put it on a suitable cable and point it somewhere else (believe me, I know what that sounds like). But it does work, and it's simple and cheap.

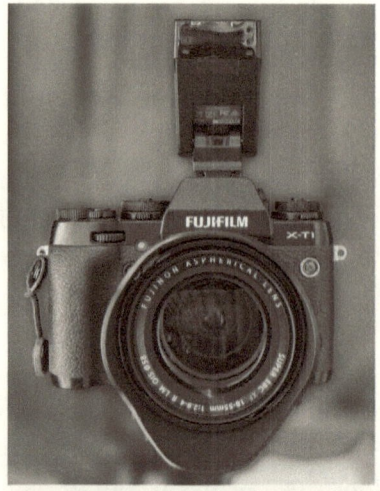

Old timers often use a piece of, *overexposed*, developed film. This is fairly easy to come by, and cuts *most* visible light while allowing infrared to pass through to cause triggering. A leftover *underexposed* piece of film works almost as well too (**Figure 7-11**), and blocks virtually *all* visible light from the flash since it's so dark.

Of course, you could put your hand, or a piece of cardboard between the master flash and your subject so there's no direct light path into the composition. If you do this, make sure the trigger pulse can still bounce its way to your slave flashes. And watch your eyes! Backwards is the most likely direction this light will take.

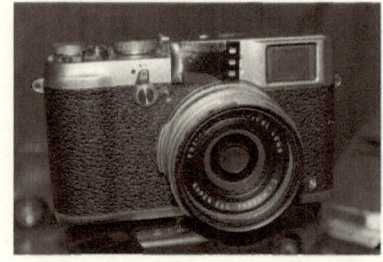

*Figure 7-11: A simple strip of underexposed, developed film makes for an ideal IR filter for your flash.*

I don't use IR triggering for off-camera flash too often, preferring what is up next:

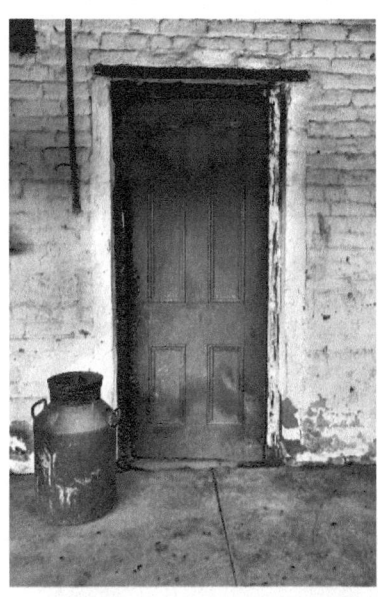

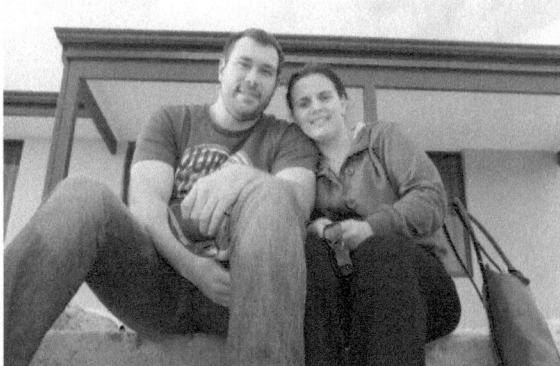

**TIP: Take your flash everywhere.** *I don't want to mislead you (by my examples) into thinking wireless flash is for studio work only. Nothing could be further from the truth. Take your wireless flash everywhere.* **Above**: *Even snap shots can look better with flash!*

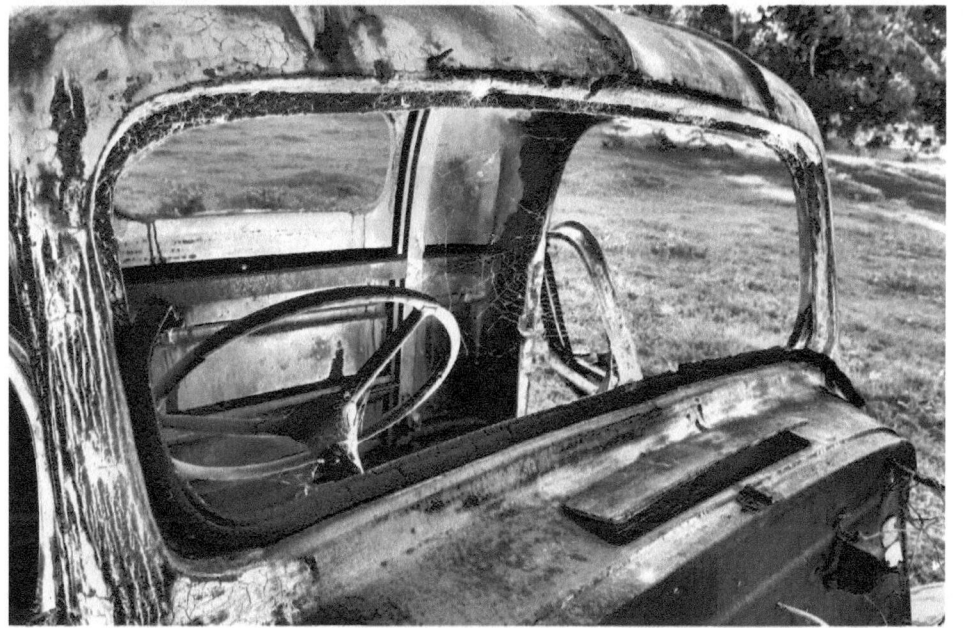

*Wireless flash (inside the cabin) and the Dynamic Tone ADV Filter.*

## RADIO WIRELESS TRIGGERING

Another really good way to separate your flash and camera is by using wireless radio triggering. As with optical IR triggering, flash output must be controlled manually.

The main benefits of wireless triggering are:

- You don't need line of sight (you can put triggers and flashes inside softboxes, or around corners and use "hidden" flashes;
- They work reliably over greater distances;
- They aren't impacted by sunlight like IR is, so are good for outdoor shoots; and
- No wires to trip over.

Cons are:

- Additional cost, and yet more kit;
- Not all triggers sync at high shutter speeds;
- No triggers give TTL exposure. Flash exposure must be calculated manually.

Most pros will recommend you use high-quality radio triggers like Pocket Wizards. These units have proven reliability and interoperability between new and old kit – which is a good thing given the investment required. Oftentimes you'll hear something like "Real pros use these.". Or, "Cheap units are an "entry tax" on people too .......... (fill in the blank) to get the good stuff.".

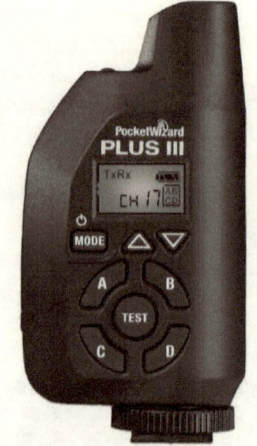

At the risk of being stoned, my take on photography is *it ain't the kit that takes the picture*. So whatever works for you - including your budget - well and good. Since I neither sell, nor am sponsored by any manufacturer, I have no axe to grind on any of it.

*Figure 7-12: The hugely popular Pocket Wizard Plus III radio transceiver (trigger and receiver).*

So way back, when I wanted more off-camera light and a radio trigger that didn't look almost as big as my camera, I purchased a Yongnuo 560 III flash (with inbuilt receiver) and tiny Yn-603C II radio transceiver (trigger and receiver) all for around $100. Since then I've added several more flashes to this kit. Incidentally, this setup cost way less than the same outlay in triggers and strobes for my DSLRs, and I couldn't be more pleased with the results. In fact, *the whole thing cost less than half* what one branded flash of similar power output will set you back!

This kit will suit most kinds of radio wireless photography you can pull off with an X-platform (or most other cameras), and is a great tool to explore your creative lighting urge without breaking the bank.

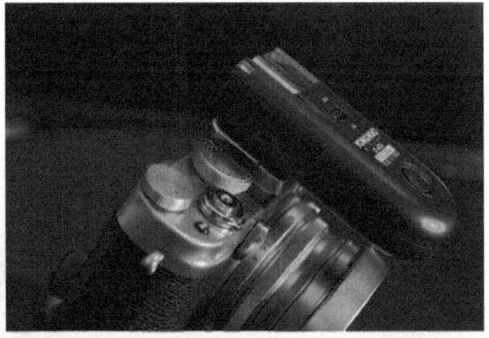

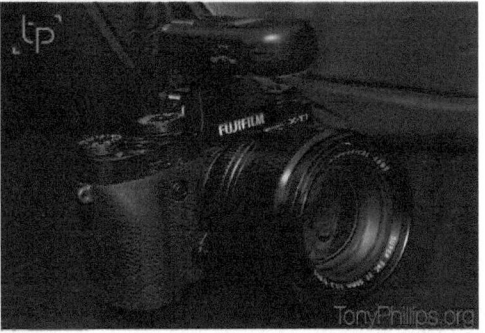

The whole thing has worked reliably, the flash units are consistent, and the little trigger is uber discrete atop the camera. Since then, I've also used these Yn flashes with DSLRs, and been pleased with the outcome. Actually, on this point, I've also done this the other way round, successfully using DSLR branded flashes with the Yn radio transceivers and XE, XT, and X100/S cameras. It works perfectly! In fact, you can use any flash this way so long as it has manual exposure mode. You can even mount the EF-X20 on a radio receiver if you want!

*Figure 7-13:* Here's a few self-referential wireless flash shots of wireless flash triggers on X-platform cameras. *Top:* The tiny Yongnuo 603c II will happily trigger manual flashes at quite high shutter speeds on the leaf shutter cameras.

Rather than bore you with the details of how to set up any particular kit, let me give some generic instructions that will work for most wireless radio setups.

1. Turn off the camera. This is important when mating radio receivers to cameras. You don't want odd things happening when you slide the trigger onto the hot shoe.

2. Attach a radio trigger to your camera, and receiver to each flash. (A Yn-603 compatible receiver is inbuilt in the Yn-560 III flash units). You can use as many flashes as you have receivers in this arrangement.

3. Turn on the wireless devices (trigger *and* receiver(s)) and put them on the same radio channel so they can communicate successfully. This process will vary from brand to brand, and it's up to you and the manual to work it out. Remember, if you're shooting in a crowd and other photographers have the same triggers, you need to use different channels to avoid firing each other's flashes.

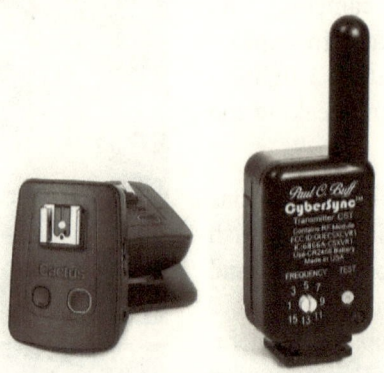

*Figure 7-14: A brace of Cactus v5 transceivers (left) and the Cybersync transmitter (right). (Not to scale.)*

4. Turn on the camera and set the flash mode to "Commander Flash" In essence, the camera is now treating your transmitter like a flash and sending the "Fire!" signal to it. Some "X" cameras need to be set to "External Flash" instead for this to work. This prevents their built in flash from firing yet sends a "Fire!" command to the transmitter on the camera's hot shoe.

5. Place slave flash(es) anywhere in the room. No need to worry about line of sight so long as you don't stick one of them in a Faraday cage.

6. Put the flash(es) in M (manual mode), and set a power output for correct exposure for each flash unit you're using. (I'll explain how to

set exposure in the next section). Power output on the Yn-560 ranges from Full (1), to 1/128 power.

7.  You're ready to shoot!
8.  Once you're done, return the camera's flash setting to "Forced Flash" so it all works as expected the next time you grab your camera.

Once you've used this setup, you'll find yourself wondering why it ever seemed difficult before. It's simple, effective, and my additional lighting kit was so cheap, and so small that I've found myself using it quite a bit. You can use as many flashes as you like in this arrangement, and any unit that will connect to a receiver and do manual flash, will do the job.

Here is a short list of radio wireless trigger systems that are reputed to work with the X-platform cameras. Some of these units reportedly sync at high shutter speeds for use with the X100/S/T. But if that's what you're after, do your research first.

A word of caution: I haven't tested most of these units, so do more research before you decide to jump in.

* Pocket Wizard PlusX or Plus III
* Cactus v5
* Cowboy Studio
* Yongnuo 603C II or 622c
* Radio Popper JRX
* Cybersync

This list is by no means exhaustive. There are yet other radio systems you could investigate.

---

**Tip 1:** *If you're tempted to grab some Yongnuo wireless triggers, make sure you get the **603C II**. This unit has a small TX-TRX switch on the side of the unit* 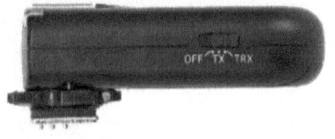 *(pictured). The original 603C does not – and while it will work with an X100/S it won't work with the X-T1 (and possibly future "X" cameras) without some soldering – which just isn't worth the effort.*

*The Yonguo 506 III unit (with compatible inbuilt wireless receiver) is designed to work with these triggers.*

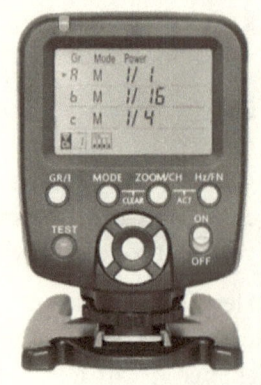

*Tip 2*: *If you get really carried away, and decide to use multiple YN 560 III flashes, here's a piece of kit you could well be interested in – the **Yongnuo 560-TX**. This device is about the size of the lower half of a 560 flash unit, and mounts on the camera, allowing you to remotely control the power output of up to 6 groups of manual flash units.*

*If you've used groups of manual flashes much, you understand that changing flash power of even a few strobes can be a bugbear – especially if they are inside softboxes. Now you can do it all right from your camera. So simple and easy to use, and it works rather well with the X-platform cameras I've tried it with.*

## COMING UP...

Up next we look at how to get manual flash exposure right! Every time!

And it is nowhere near as hard as many people think it is.

# CHAPTER 8     MANUAL FLASH MODE

With the advent of automatic TTL wireless flash exposure, why would you ever need manual control over your flash? Well, of course, with the X100S there can be no wireless triggering (either IR or radio) without manual flash. But is there any other reason for using it?

And the answer is, yes, there is. In fact such good ones that many photographers only *ever* use manual flash exposure. The picture in **Figure 8-1** is a great example of why you would use manual flash.

Automatic TTL flash works much the same as the camera's automatic exposure algorithms. In our **Figure 8-1** example, the camera's TTL flash metering would try to render the background 18% grey - remember, that's what it's programmed to think is "proper" exposure. But of course in this case, it is not. We want black to be black. And

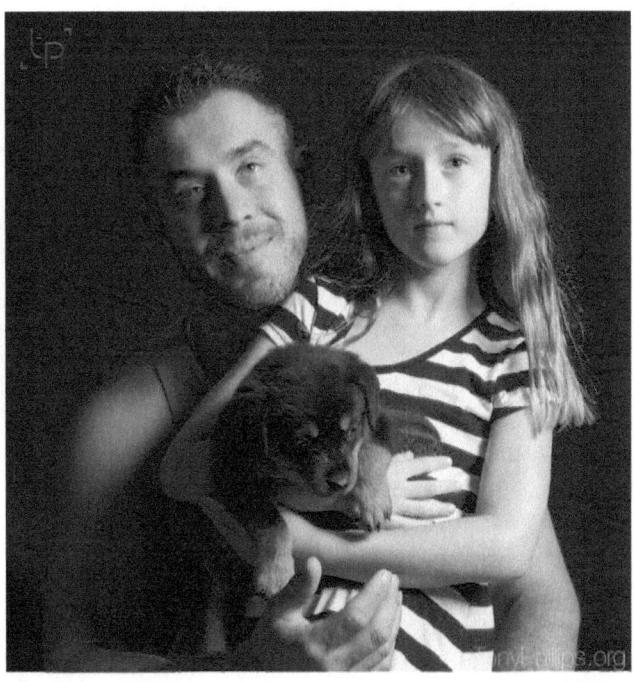

**Figure 8-1**  *Just like manual exposure mode is necessary for non-average subjects, manual mode for your flash is necessary for black (or white) backgrounds. I got this result with just one flash and one diffuser. This image was **only** cropped (slightly) and resized for the book. No post processing of any kind.*

we already know that if we were taking this picture without flash, we'd need to dial our exposure compensation down (probably by 1 stop or more) to retain the blacks and get a desirable exposure. Well, in TTL flash mode, you do much the same – dialing down *flash compensation* for exactly the same reason.

## USING A FLASHMETER TO DETERMINE EXPOSURE

If you were shooting the image in **Figure 8-1** with manual flash (which is what I actually did), you could do what photographers have done for a long time, and use a handheld exposure meter (a flashmeter) like the one pictured in **Figure 8-2**, to measure light falling on the subject. Using its exposure calculation you'd sidestep this whole auto-calculated, 18% grey, exposure business altogether. And it's for this exact reason people still use them.

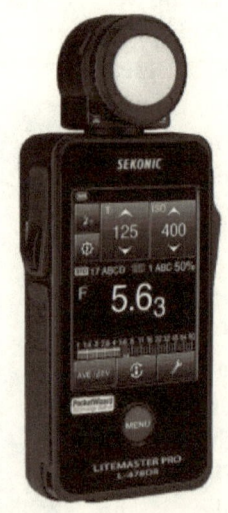

A flashmeter is a simple device to use. You enter your desired ISO and shutter speed, then test fire the manual flash(es) while holding the meter up to your subject (usually the face). The meter reads incoming light from the flash and calculates an f/stop that will get you perfect exposure irrespective of background colours, reflective properties of your

*Figure 8-2   My flashmeter. I choose ISO and shutter speed. The meter calculates f/stop based on incoming light from my flash.*

subject etc. (We talked more about this in Chapter 2.)

If you don't like a particular exposure/depth of field combination, no worries. Just alter shutter speed or ISO on the meter to arrive at a combo you do like. Now set these readings in your camera in manual exposure mode, and shoot away! As long as the *subject to flash distance* does not change, you are free to keep shooting without altering anything. You can even move camera angle or distance! In fact, you could change models, and as long as they are in the same location, exposure will still be perfect.

Using a flashmeter works whether your flash is inside a softbox, reflected off an umbrella, or pointing directly at your subject (which is generally unadvisable). All the meter cares about is the light *arriving* at the subject. It doesn't care *how* it got there, or what you did to diffuse it along the way. The Sekonic lightmeter pictured even has a version which has an inbuilt Pocket Wizard trigger which is useful for test-firing flashes right from the meter! Pretty cool – and a great time saver when you are working in a studio under the usual deadlines.

Of course, the only downside to this is additional cost. Though some perfectly serviceable pre-owned units can be had on the internet for half the cost of new.

---

**Manual Flash Tip:** *Need to fine tune the exposure using manual flash? Try moving your flash a foot or two closer, or further away from your subject, and see what difference that makes.*

*For a* **bare** *GN 58 flash on 1/8 power, going from 8ft (2.4mt) to 6ft (1.8mt) will increase light reaching your subject by approximately 2/3rds of a stop of light. (Experiment to see what your flash does in this situation. It'll be a good starting point for future manual flash work).*

---

## USING THE HISTOGRAM TO DETERMINE EXPOSURE

For a photographer on a budget, there's another way to set manual flash output though. In fact, budget or not, learning to read your camera's histogram is a perfectly viable alternative to using a flashmeter. And it's simple. Just do test shots and look at the playback histogram to see if blacks are as black as you want, and whites are properly white. If your highlights and lowlights are within range, and not clipped, you have the result you are looking for. (See Appendix A for a full discussion on interpreting the histogram – including its application to manual flash photography).

This method will work best if you establish what your starting points are – something you can easily do with a few test shots. *What you want to end up with is an understanding of how much power you typically need at a fixed distance (I use 8ft as a standard) to create a correctly exposed image.*

Here's how in a few simple steps:

- Grab a willing volunteer as your subject.
- Set your camera at ISO 800, 1/180th of a second and F/4.5. This is just a starting point. Don't adjust it throughout these tests. Adjust your flash instead. Testing should be in a low-light environment where your flash contributes 90% or more of the light.
- Put your *bare* flash on a stand about 8ft away (2.4mt) from your volunteer, and set it at 1/8[¥] power and fire off a test shot.
- Check the histogram. If it is bunched up to the right or left of the graph, simply adjust *flash power* as necessary. (See **Figure 8-3**.)
- If it is overexposed try dialing flash power down to 1/16. Lower power means faster recharge times, and less wear and tear on both flash and batteries. So start by lowering power if you can.
- If it's underexposed, you can dial up to 1/4 power.
- Record your distance:power findings, and retain this for your records.

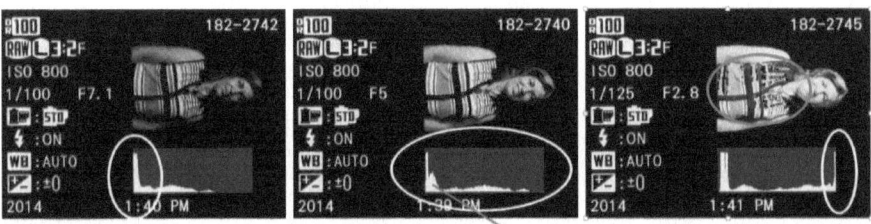

**Left**: The histogram is bunched left, indicating I'm losing blacks. **Centre**: The exposure I'm looking for. The histogram still has a spike on the left, but notice it's now not quite at the left side, showing I'm preserving detail in the black background. The graph is more evenly spread across the image showing better exposure. The spike toward the left (see large view for more detail) shows my subject darks are not underexposed, and I'm not losing much in the background either. **Right**: Now there's a spike on the right too, indicating overexposure and loss of detail in the whites. I've shown the "clipping" view the display shows you. All that dark "clipping" is really blown out whites. Not what I want at all.

**Figure 8-3** The playback histogram (Detail Info screen).

Once you have the distance:power ratio for your particular flash, it's time for some refinement. Follow these steps:

- Now move the flash 2ft closer to your subject (6ft or 1.8mt) to discover how much *more light* you get by getting the flash a measured distance closer. It makes quite a difference, doesn't it! $2/3^{rds}$ of a stop (*approx.) for average high power flash units.
- Now test how much *less light* you get by putting it 2ft further *away* (10ft or 3mt). Approx. 1/2 a stop this time!
- Record these measurements. They are very useful in fine-tuning exposure.

(*Numbers are indicative of a GN 58 flash.)

So when I mentioned adjusting flash power "as necessary", you can now see that *moving your flash toward or away from the subject is a valid exposure adjustment* in managing manual flash exposure. In fact, I often find it far easier to simply move the flash stand a little forwards or backwards to fine tune exposure, rather than change power settings on the flash, or adjusting ISO or aperture settings in the camera.

If you use light modifiers like softboxes or umbrellas (which I recommend - and discuss in the next section), try the whole exercise again, and record how much light they *each eat up*. Perhaps around $1/3^{rd}$ of a stop for a 43" silver umbrella, and around 2½ stops for a medium diffused softbox – though each diffuser will vary somewhat. You will want to record this number for each modifier you use.

Once you have this collection of lighting data, it'll be easy from here on out to adequately judge where to start with manual lighting, *and* you'll be able to confidently plonk your flash down about 8ft from the subject, set your camera exposure to those known numbers, set the appropriate power setting on the flash (from your recorded data), add a softbox or umbrella, and fire a test shot – all with reasonable certainty that you're in the exposure ballpark. A few tweaks from there, and you're done!

Whatever results you get from your testing will depend entirely on the flash you use. 1/8 power on a GN 20 flash is nothing like 1/8 power on a GN 58 flash. All my examples are based on the assumption that your flash is a camera-branded main flash model, or a similarly powered third-party flash like the Yn-560 (which is GN 58). Your results will obviously vary if this is not the case.

In fact, if you have a collection of notably different flash units, or just want to be precise, test all of them as I've described, recording data for each. Certainly, if you have GN20, GN42, and GN58 flashes in your kit bag they need to be "ranged" individually since their full power output is so varied.

You might imagine that if you're using a flashmeter, there's no need to do any of this testing. But if you do, you'll have the same confident starting point in establishing manual flash exposure, and you'll understand thoroughly the relationship between the exposure variables once you've completed the exercise. So go ahead – do it anyway.

## OTHER EXPOSURE VARIABLES

Since flash is not the only exposure variable in play when shooting manual flash, you might wonder how other camera exposure controls (ISO, shutter speed, and aperture) impact on manual flash exposure.

**ISO**: I usually set ISO as low as is practical given lighting conditions. Since I'm using flash, it's usually not too bothersome to keep it low – but it is a variable. If you run out of flash power, and cannot get your lights closer to your subject, increase ISO sensitivity. And next time, bring more light! ☺

**Aperture** plays exactly the same role in flash exposure. Adjusting it up (using a smaller aperture number) will let more light through. Though since it also plays a key role in depth of field, you might like to start with this creative choice first. I used F/4.5 in my "ranging" method above, simply as an average aperture with a reasonable depth of field - and because many lenses perform better (sharper) if they are *not* used at their maximum or minimum apertures.

**Shutter speed**, on the other hand, does *NOT* alter flash exposure. And the reason for this is the speed of the flash pulse is *at least* an order of magnitude higher than the fastest flash sync speed the camera can manage. If you have an X100 series camera, you will be aware that you can take flash images at quite high shutter speeds ($1/2000^{th}$ according to the manual). What's happening here is the high shutter speed controls the exposure for *ambient light* (just as it would if no flash was used), and the added flash pulse (still quite a bit faster than $1/2000^{th}$ of a second) briefly lights the foreground to increase exposure in just that area of the picture. (There's much more on this topic in Chapter 11, and even if you do not own one of these cameras, you might find it stimulating to read. Additionally, there's more on the relationship between aperture, shutter speed, depth of field, etc in Appendix B.)

OK. To summarize, there are four variables which impact on manual flash exposure:

- Power output of the flash (from full power down to $1/128^{th}$ power)

- Distance between the flash and the subject
- Aperture setting
- ISO setting

Any of these can be used to control exposure using manual flash.

## COMING UP...

A simple way to create drama with light – a quick look at the lighting technique known as "ratio lighting".

# CHAPTER 9    CREATING    DRAMA    WITH RATIO LIGHTING

You might have noticed the lighting in my example images is *never* from the front, and rarely consistently even across my subjects. Professional portrait photographers and cinematographers know that the most flattering and dramatic lighting for people is "ratio lighting", where you have *two* lights illuminating your subject – one from the left, another to the right, with one of these lights being stronger than the other. **Figure 10-6** and **Figure 9-2** show examples of "ratio lighting" (where one light is *much* stronger than the other). A widely acceptable ratio in use is 2:1.

There are two simple ways to do 2:1 ratio lighting:
1. Place two lights equal distances, one either side of your subject, and make the power of one twice the other (see **Figure 9-1**), or,
2. Place one light twice as far away as the other with the same power setting.

Painless, huh!

Want some other ratio? Just move the light stand some more! ☺ I jest. But that's an easy way to get the job done.

In reality though, precise ratio lighting is somewhat more complex than described above. And the reason for this is that light does not fall off in a linear fashion. So to be accurate, what

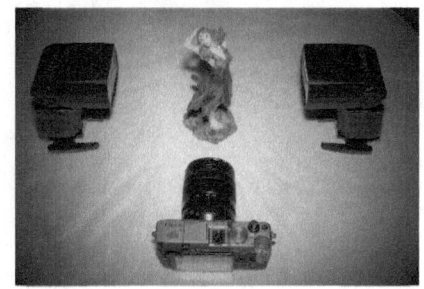

*Figure 9-1: Ratio lighting diagram using two flashes! For fun I shot this with the Toy Camera filter.*

we really want for 2:1 lighting (often used for female portraits) is one stop of light difference between the two flashes, no matter how they are placed. 4:1 lighting (often used for male portraits), requires a two stop difference between main and fill lights – and 8:1 ratio lighting requires three stops difference.

Of course, if you don't have a way to measure the contribution of each of your flashes, and don't want to learn the math involved for accurate placement, you can go back to where I started this chapter, and place your lights in approximate locations, and fine tune from there, checking your histogram to ensure it is doing what you want from your image.

If you don't have two flashes, you can still do ratio lighting. Use light from a nearby window (and a diffuser if needs be to soften it), or reflectors as I've done in some of my examples. White card makes excellent reflectors.

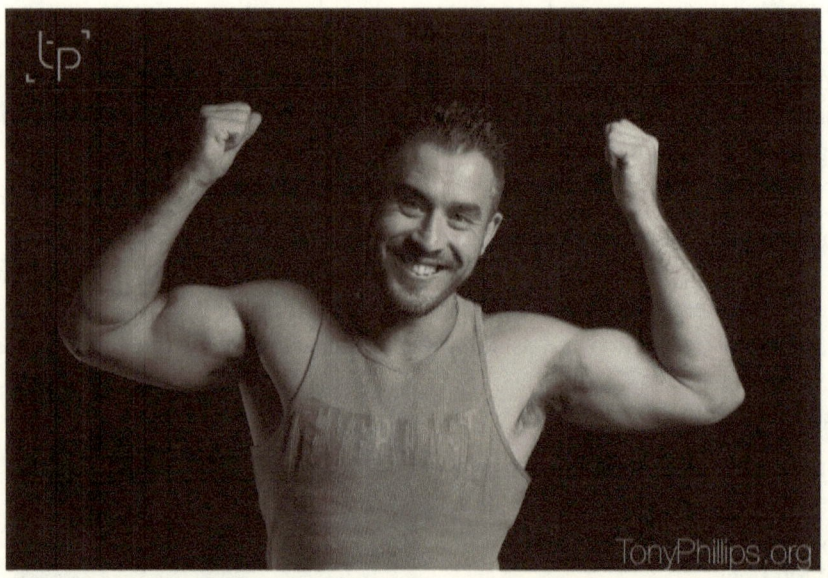

**Figure 9-2:** *An invigorating example of high ratio lighting. There's a tiny rim light off to the left at quite low power to lift and define detail where I wanted it.*

In studios, photographers often use quite complex ratio lighting, employing hair lights above a model on a boom arm; managing directional control with grids on softboxes; or by using precisely controlled rim (or other) lights to light just a portion of the composition to get the desired effect.

Ratio lighting is another great way to create memorable images.

<u>COMING UP...</u>

How to use light modifiers to improve the quality of your light. And I show you my portable lighting kit.

# CHAPTER 10    LIGHT MODIFIERS

We've looked at getting the flash away from the camera to improve quality of light. Now let's take that a step further by considering how we modify this off-camera light for maximum effect.

Pictures are really 2D flat images, right? But by controlling how your compositions is lit, you can bring an alluring 3D quality to these 2D images. Bouncing light off ceilings, pieces of paper, or flip-it like commercial reflectors is nice if you're out in the field, or a photojournalist, but if you want to "paint" your composition with high quality diffused light, you have to turn to the kind of tools professionals have been using for ages to modify their light. Unfortunately, there seems to be hundreds of choices! But the two most common (and effective) light modifiers, are umbrellas and softboxes. Throw in a reflector or two, and you round out your lighting kit nicely.

These types of light modifiers are used to 1) *control light direction*, and 2) *soften light* to give pleasing shadows – while adding 3-D dimensionality to an image. **Figure 10-1** shows you what I mean.

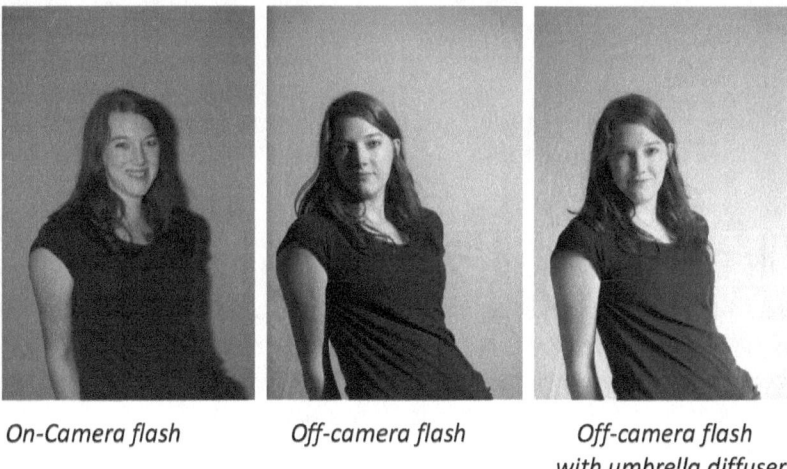

On-Camera flash        Off-camera flash        Off-camera flash
                                               with umbrella diffuser

*Figure 10-1:* *Off-camera flash with light modifiers really makes a difference!! The same flash used three different ways demonstrates what I mean.*

## UMBRELLAS & SOFTBOXES

So where do you start? Soft box maybe, or umbrella? Both create great light. **Figure 10-2** shows a model with both modifiers. The quality of the light is good in both (though slightly different).

So if you're just starting into lighting, or want to experiment with your camera and a flash, a reflective umbrella is a pretty good option. It is cheaper (by far), and generally much easier to set up than most softboxes. And it is easier to carry too!

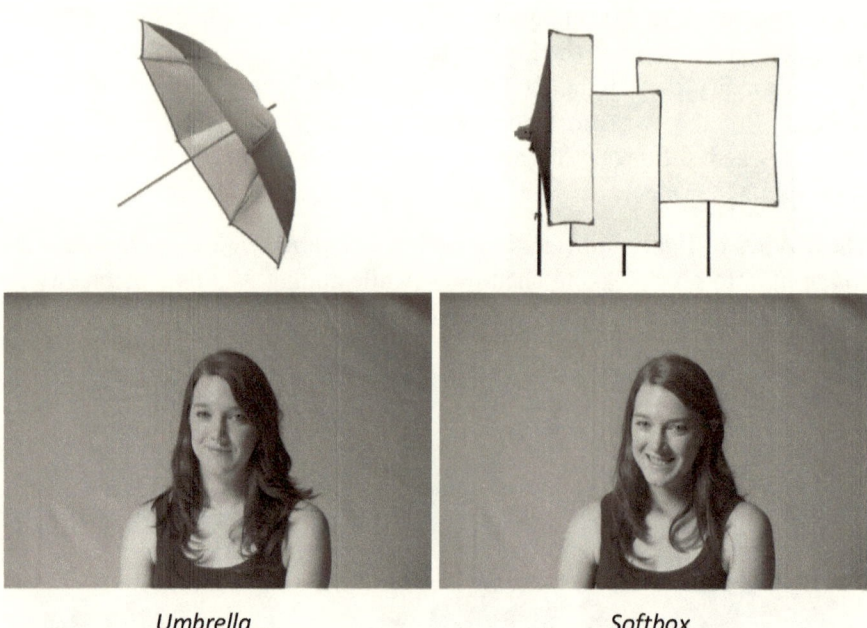

*Umbrella*          *Softbox*

**Figure 10-2:** *A comparison of an umbrella (left) and a softbox (right). The softbox tends to produce softer light, but is also about 3x more expensive. The relative difference in the shadow on the model's face is accounted for because I used a 48" umbrella, and only a 28" softbox (see upcoming tip).*

Here again, there are so many umbrellas to choose from. Some have silver reflectors. Others gold (I'd avoid these as a starter, since it will warm the image considerably). There are also translucent "shoot-through" umbrellas made of sheer white fabric (See **Figure 10-3**). Instead of using these as a reflector, you point your flash into them with the model on the other side.

They are great for getting good light quite close to your subject, since there's no shaft protruding to skewer the unwary model. Flash power can be lower in this usage since you are closer to the subject.

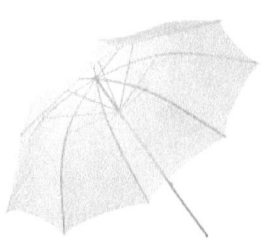

If you shop right, you might grab a dual purpose umbrella – both reflector *and* a shoot through in one. See my notes a few sections on for a recommendation.

*Figure 10-3:* *A typical shoot-through translucent umbrella.*

So why a softbox? Well, square "catchlights", for one. Some people like the "glint" in their subject's eyes to mimic window light, and rectangular softboxes do this better than round umbrellas. They don't spill light everywhere like umbrellas, either. And you can easily attach directional modifiers (grids) to the front of softboxes – though soft box light is considerably more directional than umbrella light anyway.

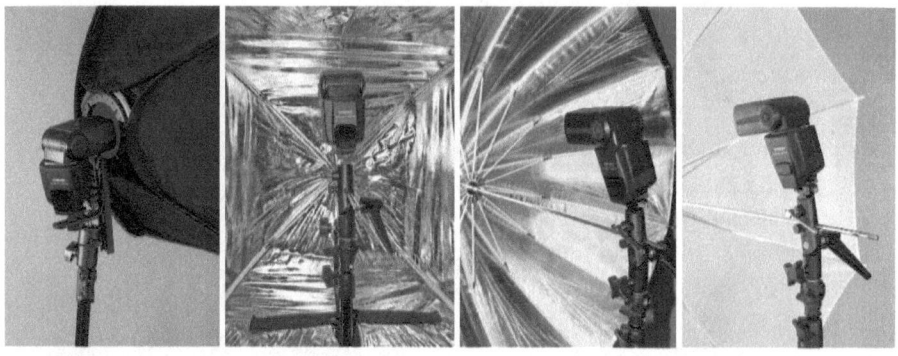

Regular Softbox        Umbrella Softbox           Silver Umbrella    Shoot Thru Umbrella

*Figure 10-4:* *Using IR wireless triggering? For maximum reliability, rotate the flash body so that the IR sensor is facing **something** that reflects the "Fire!" signal to it. Signal can reflect off your subject (as with the umbrella softbox) or arrive more directly from the camera (other images).*

There are softboxes that fold rapidly like umbrellas (see **Figure 10-4b**), but buy from a reputable manufacturer, and they run to four times the price of an umbrella! But be warned. If the lighting bug bites, there'll come a day when a quick-fold softbox will hit the top of your shopping list for sure!

If you're using IR optical triggering to fire your wireless flash inside softboxes or umbrellas, you're likely to experience issues with accurate triggering since there's not always line of sight between the master flash (camera) and slave flashes. Of course, many flash units allow you to rotate the flash head. This way you can direct the flash beam into the softbox/umbrella but still have the flash IR sensor pointing outwards where it can get a trigger signal. (**Figure 10-4**).

---

*Size Matters: Photographers know the size of a light diffuser is more important than if it's an umbrella, softbox, or shoot-through. **The larger the surface, the softer the light.** The larger the diffuser, the more light wraps round the subject!*

---

## REFLECTORS

Don't forget the humble reflector in all this. This is really like a portable white wall or ceiling you can place wherever you want. Pair it with a wireless flash, and you can create quite effective results. The picture in **Figure 10-5** was taken with a single wireless flash and one reflector. The setting sun was golden to the left of shot, and the reflector was about 30 degrees to the right. The flash was pointing *AT* the reflector.

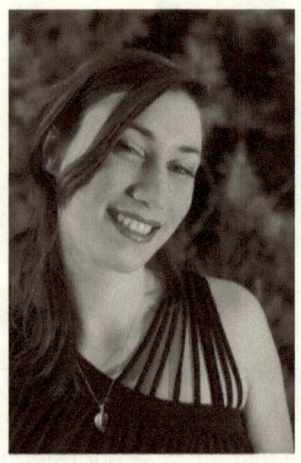

Reflectors come in various sizes and typically collapse into bundles you can pack in a small bag. My largest "portable" reflector measures 7ft by 5ft. Mind you, I have also used white sign board as reflectors when I needed

*Figure 10-5 This picture was taken with a single wireless flash, and a white reflector.*

something. Visit a signage print shop and they probably have tons of useful offcuts they'll give you. 5 in 1 foldable reflectors are also available quite cheaply – and unless you're planning to use them professionally, the cheapest ones will give you good service for quite a while.

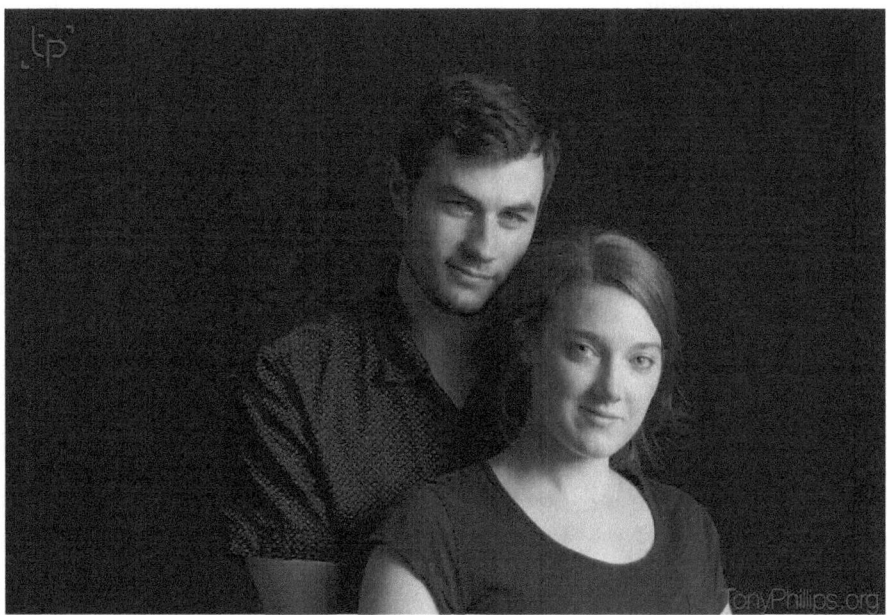

**Figure 10-6:** *An umbrella (and light stand), one flash, and a black backdrop is all you need to create professional-looking portraits. A black sheet works well, or you can buy cheap (yet serviceable) stands and backdrops online starting at about $60.*

**Distance Matters**: *It isn't just size that affects light from softboxes and umbrellas.* **The closer the light is to the subject, the softer it becomes.** *Conversely, the further away it is, the harder it becomes.*

## AN ULTRA-PORTABLE STUDIO SET UP

It doesn't matter who you ask, everyone will have a different "go" bag.

**Figure 10-7** shows the kit in my ultra-portable studio. It uses just one wireless flash and a diffusing umbrella. Here's a parts list:

- A Westcott satin (#2011) double-fold umbrella. This serves as both a reflector, and a shoot-through if I remove the outer black cover, so I get added flexibility wherever I go. *AND*, it collapses to under 15"!

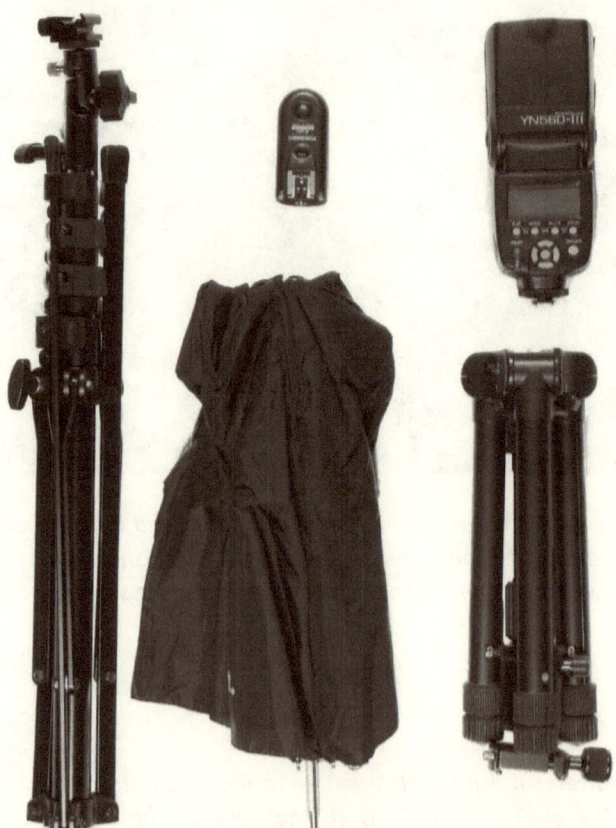

*Figure 10-7*: *The kit, the whole kit, and nothing but the kit! Well, this and a black sheet, for a backdrop. Use the flash unit as some indication of just how small this kit really is! The umbrella furls tight like a regular briefcase umbrella.*

- Portable light stand. (7ft Hobo Lighting 5 Section CLS65Pro). There are several great light-weight, light stands. My stand came from CotswoldPhoto on ebay UK. It doesn't always go with me. My pack-muling (I think that's a word ☺) days are over!
- Umbrella mounting hardware (pictured atop the stand).
- One flash. (Yn-560 III and 603c transceiver / trigger in this case). You can use any flash and trigger / triggering system.
- A lightweight tripod. (Velbon Ultrek 43DL). If the job is local, I lug one of my studio tripods.
- Black cloth for backdrop (black bed sheets work well and are cheap).
- A brace of ultra-cheap bags to cart it in (not pictured).
- Sometimes I add a second flash.

I usually position the umbrella about 45 degrees to one side (as in the image in **Figure 8-1** and others), but 90 degrees works too, depending on the subject. **Figure 10-8** shows an example of this.

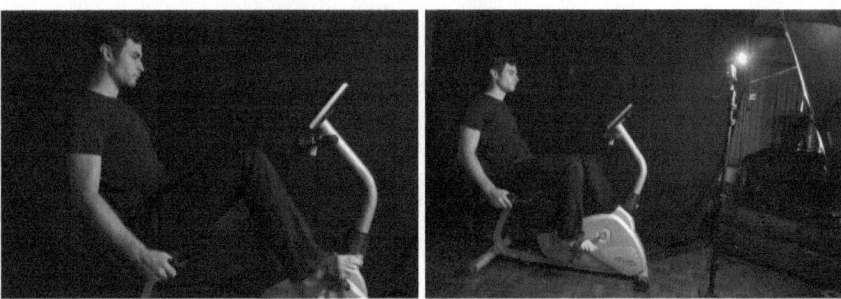

*Figure 10-8*: My go-anywhere 1-flash studio is simple, yet produces outstanding results.

I've mentioned the Westcott 43" Optical White Satin, collapsible (double fold), reflective umbrella (#2011) with removable cover. I like it mostly for the soft, wrapping quality of light. But it's tiny too, and multi-tasking since I can strip the black cover off and use it as a shoot-through umbrella. All this is good for light-weight travel.

Sounds perfect, right? But beware, if you buy one, the cover *will* pop off at the *slightest* provocation, and actually slow you down! To fix this, grab some thin shirring elastic from a fabric shop (approx. $1/16^{th}$ inch – or 1.5mm diameter), and tie a loop as demonstrated in **Figure 10-9**.

Westcott manufacture a 45" satin umbrella with all the same features and benefits in a standard fold – so it's not as tiny when folded, but you won't have the problem I've describe with the cover. It all depends on your shooting and travel requirements – the elastic fix isn't hard to do if you decide to go for the collapsible unit.

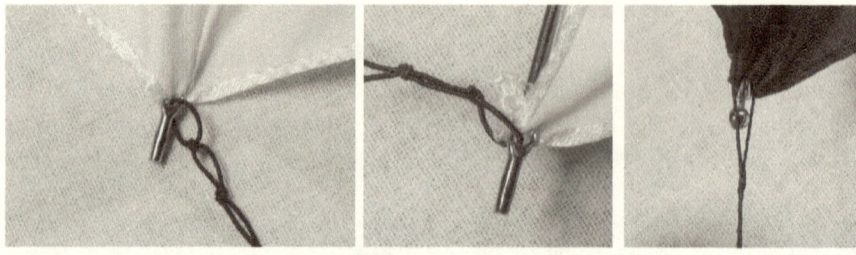

**Figure 10-9**: *You'll be more inclined to use the tiny 43in Westcott #2011 pictured in **Figure 10-7** if you make these even tinier retaining loops from shirring elastic. Just hook them over the rib-ends to hold the black cover in place. This is quick and easy to do, and will save much muttering and mumbling. Trust me on this!*

---

**Kit Tip:** *The Velbon tripod pictured in **Figure 10-7** is not only light, but will easily hold 3.5kg (any fully loaded X-platform camera). I purchased the 40L legs, and added a very smooth PhotoClam PC-33NS Ballhead (arca-swiss). The whole thing is tiny and weighs under 1.2kg (2.4lb).*

---

*Tip:* When shooting with manual exposure "M" mode and manual flash as described in the previous sections, there's a menu item you're going to want to turn off: **Exp. In Manual Mode → Off**.

Since the camera doesn't know about the manual flash (or at least how much light it will contribute to the exposure), it makes no allowance for it at all when displaying the preview. In practice, this means your LCD/EVF will be so dark, you won't be able to see to focus accurately, or compose your picture with any certainty. Turn this setting "Off", and the viewfinder won't show the exposure preview. **Note:** the exact behavior of this function varies a bit from camera to camera. At the time of this writing, the X100S (for instance) will still show you exposure preview after you've locked exposure by half-pressing the shutter button – making it awfully difficult to focus-recompose if that's what you're doing. The X-T1 turns preview off, assuming you are completely in charge of your flash exposure.

Turn this menu option "On" again when you're not using manual flash, to get a clearer indication of what's happening with your exposure. This setting has no effect in P, A, or S modes.

COMING UP...

That was fun. Now let's jump into something X100 series owners will find really juicy!

Plus we discuss how focal plane shutters work, and what's behind 1/180th as the max sync speed for interchangeable lens "X" cameras.

# CHAPTER 11    X100 SERIES FLASH - REAL HIGH SPEED SYNC (RHSS)

A select few of the Fujifilm X-platform cameras have a very special ability that delivers flash images unobtainable in most cameras. And if you're lucky enough to own one, you will really want to experiment with its high speed flash syncing.

In the pursuit of great images, *quality* of light is far more important than *quantity* of light. So if it's quality you want, the X100 series leaf shutter/ND filter/real high-speed sync combination brings you a gift-horse not to be overlooked because of its limitations (you'll understand soon).

Essentially, the leaf shutter design makes it easier to balance ambient light with flash - and you don't have to use huge studio strobes to get the job done. This means the tiny in-built GN-10) flash, or indeed the EF-X20/EF-20 (GN-20) flashes pack a flash punch far above their obvious weight.

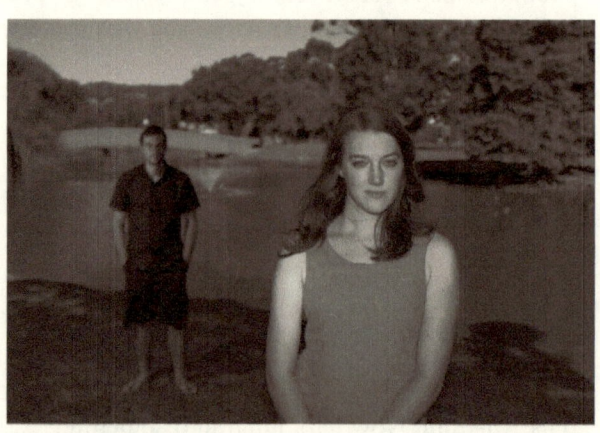

But there are some limitations - or at least factors to be aware of in using this powerful feature-pack – to get the most from it. Once I've ticked these items off for you though, you'll see why *this is the gift-horse feature you actually, really bought this camera for.* (See example **Figure 11-1**).

**Figure 11-1:** *Real High Speed Sync (RHSS) lets you shoot wide open on a sunny day (1/1,000th in this case), giving you an out-of-focus background with great foreground lighting.*
*With the ND filter "On" and my subjects in open shade, I needed two flashes to light this composition - the tiny EF-X20 atop the camera, and a manual wireless flash to lift my second subject.*

In most high-end cameras, the shutter is a physical device that momentarily exposes the sensor to light for a period determined by the chosen shutter speed. There are various kinds of shutter mechanisms, each with benefits and limitations – one of which is the maximum speed at which the mechanism actuates.

## FOCAL PLANE SHUTTERS AND HSS

Let's step aside for a second, and briefly consider how, and why shutters, and therefore, HSS (High Speed Sync) works in focal plane shutter cameras (just about every current high-end camera, *other than* the X100 series, PhaseOne (IQ+645DF), and Hasselblad (H4D-40)). Of course, you don't need to know any of this to use RHSS, but while I've deliberately oversimplified it, the following explanation may help clear up confusion between "regular" HSS, and the kind of "*on-steroids*" HSS the X100/S/T delivers – which I've dubbed Real High Speed Sync (RHSS).

Normal focal plane shutters expose a camera's sensor to light by moving a "slit" across the sensor at a fixed speed (simulated in **Figure 11-2**). This transit speed is always the same. What changes when you alter shutter speed is the *width* of the slit. (A narrow slit means a high shutter speed. A wide slit means a lower shutter speed.) What's happening, of course, is each pixel in the sensor is exposed to light for *only* the period in which the slit transits across it. So a wider slit in the shutter means more light falls on a particular pixel than would with a narrow one.

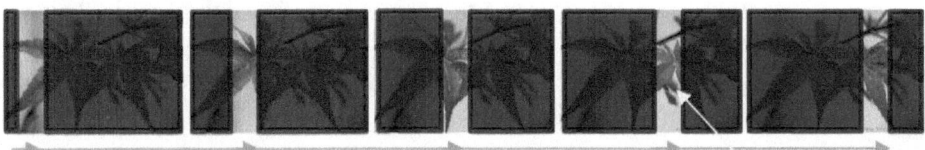

*Figure 11-2:* A simulation of a focal plane shutter in action moving left to right. Only one portion of the sensor is exposed to light at any time, and the width of the "travelling slit" is determined by the shutter speed. I've shown the shutter traversing horizontally, though many shutters traverse vertically instead.

Examine **Figure 11-2** again, imagining what would happen if the flash was to deliver its burst while the shutter was in *any* position illustrated. Only that portion of the image would be lit by the flash, right?

So clearly, the limitation with this system is that for the flash to illuminate the entire width of the sensor in one burst, *the shutter speed must be sufficiently slow enough for the slit to be as wide as the whole sensor*! Whatever this speed is, is a particular camera's maximum "flash sync speed", and will be listed in the manual. For most cameras, this speed is lower than $1/250^{th}$ of a second (you'll often see numbers like 1/125, 1/160, 1/200, and for a few cameras, 1/320 as the maximum sync speed. Interchangeable lens X-platform cameras max sync speed is $1/180^{th}$).

Enter HSS: To get around this relatively low shutter speed limitation, the flash can be "pulsed" in a long, low-intensity burst spreading light out over the entire transit of the shutter. *Meaning you can shoot with flash at much higher shutter speeds than normal* (normal being the advertised flash sync speed).

You can even use wide apertures for improved bokeh (low depth of field, background blur). But like so many other things, there's a limitation to this wonderful piece of engineering. The same *amount* of power that was previously available to deliver a single burst of light has now been used to produce the sustained lower-intensity burst across the entire sensor.

Think of it like the gas tank in a rocket. You can fire it off all at once, delivering a huge amount of power (flash, to light the entire image). Or you can use it a little at a time, producing controlled bursts (some flash for each part of the image). In the end, it's used up either way doing work. These controlled bursts mean that each portion of the sensor only gets a small amount of light – typically $1/8^{th}$ or so of the full flash power (depending on the actual shutter speed).

So your GN-58 flash is now only worth $1/8^{th}$ (approx) of its actual output when used in HSS mode! Or, to oversimplify that, but put it another way, if you wanted to deliver a full burst of flash power using HSS, you'd need 8 GN-58 flashes to deliver a single, full-power flash burst across the entire sensor using HSS!

Now I know if you are technically inclined, you will likely find this explanation overly simple. It ignores electronic first shutter, fully exposed sensors, and the like. But the approach is deliberate, and only intended to lead to the next explanation, which is how the X100 series of cameras deliver their high speed sync – and why this is hugely beneficial to us as photographers.

## HOW RHSS WORKS

The remainder of this section deals with how the X100 series shutter, and its form of HSS work.

A leaf shutter does the same job as a focal plane shutter – it exposes or protects the sensor from light. Where a focal plane shutter is essentially a curtain with an opening, traversing the sensor, a leaf shutter looks, and acts more like a lens iris (aperture), opening and closing in a somewhat similar fashion. It's not near the sensor either, but rather tucked inside the lens, not too far removed from the actual iris itself.

At one time, leaf shutters were quite popular. But they contain many moving parts, making manufacture intricate and more expensive than focal plane shutters – hence their demise.

Since I don't own any old leaf shutter cameras, I'm entirely unwilling to pull one apart to photograph for this book. But think of the shutter as a cascading scissor action, and you'll have an impression of what's going on in the X100/S/T when you press the shutter button.

### SHUTTER SPEED VS APERTURE

According to Kevin Housen (www.khousen.com), the X100S's shutter takes about 1/600th of a second to close. Kevin has a great description of how the shutter mechanism works, and some very high speed videos demonstrating the X100S's shutter in action. His conclusion from these tests is: "If it takes 1/600 of a second to close, then you can't have a wide-open aperture at shutter speeds faster than 1/600."

In practice, this doesn't seem to make much difference at shutter speeds of 1/1000th, and indeed, the X100S's manual states: "The flash will synchronize with the shutter at speeds of $1/2000^{th}$ s or slower.". A statement overlooked by those who claim it syncs at *any* shutter speed.

In fact, just like so many other things in photography (or indeed, life), there's a limiting corollary relationship - in this case, between using high shutter speeds, and wide apertures. Having said that though, you can use the flash at any *available* shutter speed.

In this case, "available / unavailable", is defined as a combination of shutter speed and aperture. Where an exposure combination is unavailable, the "offending" setting (shutter or aperture) is displayed in red along the bottom of the viewfinder instead of its otherwise cheery aqua (EVF/LCD) or white (OVF).

As an example, the following table summarizes the limitations imposed on exposure combinations by the inclusion of the leaf shutter in the X100S:

| Shutter Speed (seconds) | | | | |
|---|---|---|---|---|
| Up to 1/1000$^{th}$ | To 1/1200$^{th}$ | To 1/2000$^{th}$ | To 1/2500$^{th}$ | To 1/4000$^{th}$ |
| f/2.0 | f/2.0 | f/2.0 | f/2.0 | f/2.0 |
| f/2.8 | f/2.8 | f/2.8 | f/2.8 | f/2.8 |
| f/4 | f/4 | f/4 | f/4 | f/4 |
| f/5.6 | f/5.6 | f/5.6 | f/5.6 | f/5.6 |
| f/8 - f/16 | f/8 - f/16 | f/8 - f/16 | f/8 - f/16 | f/8 - f/16 |

*Red = unavailable combinations*

Now go ahead and manually set one of these "unavailable" exposure combinations on your camera. You'll see the red warning numbers at the bottom of the screen, but ignore them, and take a picture. Now play it back.

What do you see? Well, as long as the numbers were within normal exposure limits, I bet the picture looked pretty much like you'd expect it to. So what's going on?

Well, of these higher shutter speeds, Kevin Housen further concludes: "though you may have the aperture set to f/2 at 1/4000, the shutter is closed considerably before the flash fires", so "the aperture really isn't f/2, so don't expect the nice soft backgrounds you'd normally get from f/2.".

What he's saying is that the shutter actually contributes an aperture "effect" to the image! And high shutter speeds are effected *the most* by the size of the opening of the shutter itself as it's actuating while still capturing your image. Examine the crop (**Figure 11-3**) from the F/2.8 image in **Figure 11-4**, and you get a taste of this in action, showing a somewhat greater depth of field than you might expect from the reported aperture setting.

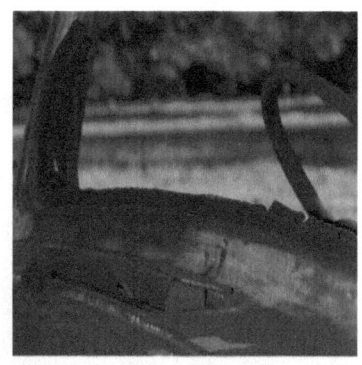

***Figure 11-3:*** *A crop from the F/2.8 image in* **Figure 11-4**.

So, for large aperture openings (like f/2), shutter speeds heading towards the camera's maximum 1/4000th second, are impacted by the physical speed of the shutter limiting the size of the shutter opening at such a high speed. Which has the effect of sharpening your images. Playing back these images on a monitor might show you this effect, depending somewhat on the background you were shooting against.

Incidentally, there's another factor at play here too. A focal plane shutter operates in close proximity to the sensor. Being inside the lens, the leaf shutter does not. Which is partly why it gives this added "aperture" effect – and also why it "works" at shutter speeds well above its mechanical maximum – since light gets through the shutter opening, reaching the entire sensor from the moment the shutter begins actuating till the instant it closes.

## *SHUTTER, APERTURE AND FLASH*

Given all this, you might well wonder what is happening when you use the flash at high shutter speeds?

Clearly, the limits of the actual shutter speed mechanism, mean the shutter cannot *really* be fully open at $1/4000^{th}$ of a second – which means a full flash pulse (which admittedly is considerably shorter than even that high shutter speed) will be partially obscured from reaching the entire sensor. You can test this light fall-off by firing your flash at something like a white wall using increasingly higher shutter speeds. But beware. You'll get the

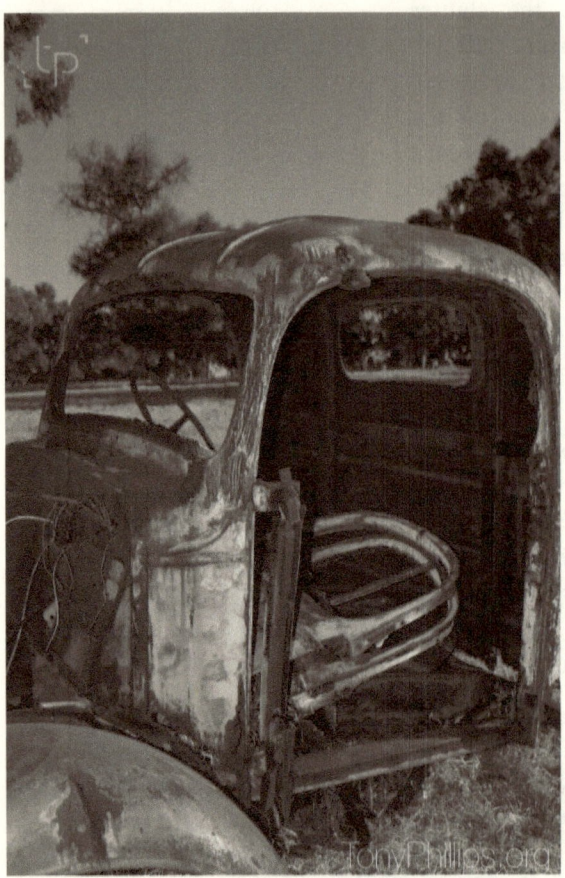

*Figure 11-4: RHSS with the EF-X20 flash. Experiment with RHSS on all kinds of subjects to see them really pop! (1/1600th, F/2.8, Velvia film, +ND)*

most accurate results if you attach the flash to the camera, or by cable to avoid wireless lag.

But what does it all mean in practical, everyday use? Well, David Hobby (strobist.com) explains it this way: "your flash has the furthest possible "ambient-mix" reach when your shutter is at 1/1000th and the aperture is at f/2".

You *can* use higher shutter speeds, but beware, you start to lose light due to the rapidly actuating shutter combined with flash firing (timing). Indeed, you'll still get quite good results at $1/2000^{th}$, though you are now aware that the background will begin to sharpen, your flash light won't "reach" as far, you'll get some light falloff at the fringes of your image, and you are now technically outside the limits of the shutter mechanism itself.

## FLASH POWER

Earlier, I mentioned one of the benefits of RHSS flash is your strobes pack a punch well above their obvious weight. Let's consider flash *power* for a moment to understand why.

If all factors effecting exposure (ISO, aperture and flash output), are equal, then keeping the shutter open for just $1/1000^{th}$ of a second vs $1/250^{th}$ of a second (for a focal plane camera), gives a 2 stop *flash* advantage! ($250 \rightarrow$ $500 \rightarrow 1000$).

Said another way, to take the same shot you can pull off with your tiny GN-20 flash unit at $1/1000^{th}$ with another focal plane camera at a max sync speed of $1/250^{th}$, requires *two stops more flash* light.

Now that probably doesn't sound like much of a big deal in this kind of example, but if you're outside wanting to balance daylight and ambient light, then GN-58 strobes are going to do a surprising job for you when paired with the X100/S/T's RHSS capability. **Figure 11-4** shows the tiny GN-20 flash is surprisingly useful in full daylight (100 degrees, 3pm, summer sun).

## NEUTRAL DENSITY – THE ND FILTER & FLASH

Before we jump into putting RHSS to work for us, let's examine another great feature of the X100 series cameras which go hand in hand with RHSS use - the inbuilt ND (Neutral Density) filter (see **Figure 11-5**).

The X100/S/T has a high-quality inbuilt 3-Stop ND filter which sits between the lens and the sensor to reduce the amount of light hitting the sensor.

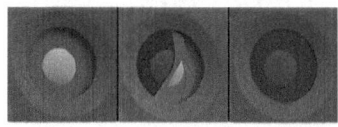

**Figure 11-5:** *Actuating the X100S's inbuilt ND filter drops a real, high-quality 3 stop ND filter in the light path.*

Typically, ND filters are most used to cut ambient light to allow slow shutter speeds – often to smooth out running water and give it a sense of movement.

Indeed, I found myself smiling recently when I heard someone describe an ND filter as "old-school". ND filters are one of the few filters I still use on a regular basis with digital cameras. And I use them for the same reason "old-school" photographers have for years: To reduce ambient light so I can have quite slow shutter speeds for induced motion blur (waterfalls etc. – see **Figure 11-6**).

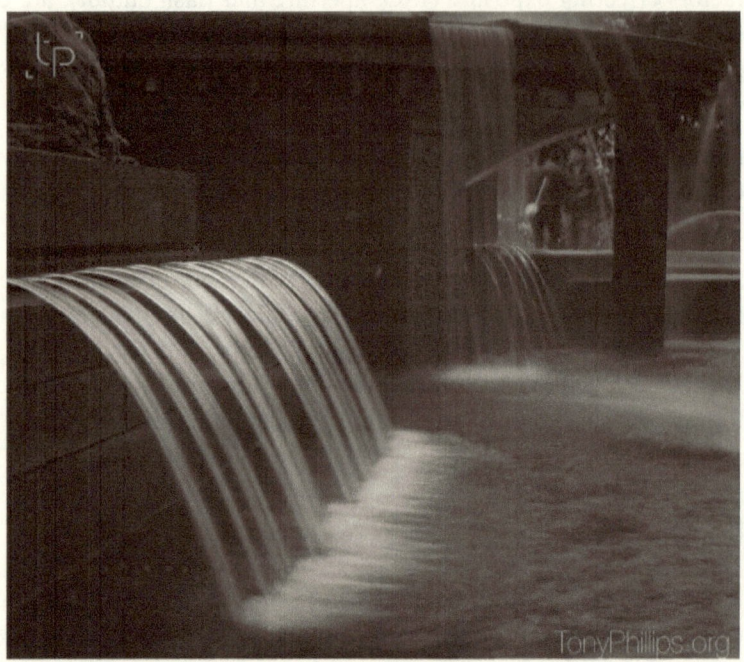

***Figure 11-6:*** *Using an ND filter to slow shutter speed for silky water effects. (And a monochrome process for fun.)*

There's another important reason to use the X100/S/T's ND filter though: You can also use it to cut ambient light to allow for both high shutter speeds *and* wide open apertures, giving you the ability to balance bright ambient daylight but keep a shallow Depth of Field.

So adding the ND filter to the mix, gives you the option to keep the shutter speed sufficiently low enough in high-ambient lighting conditions, (yet still gain control over the amount of ambient light in the exposure), all while shooting as wide open as you want for controlled depth of field (to further separate the subject from the background, creating great bokeh and three-dimensionality), all while adding a burst of flash to "pop" the subject in the foreground (see **Figure 11-7**).

This also means you can *lower* shutter speed to "sidestep" those "high shutter speed vs aperture limitations discussed earlier in this chapter. Not a bad outcome!

When a novice asks me what an ND filter is, I describe it as "sunglasses for my camera". And just as sunglasses cut light so your eyes can open wider in bright light, so too with your camera. You can open the aperture wider when your camera is wearing its ND "sunglasses". How old school is that!?

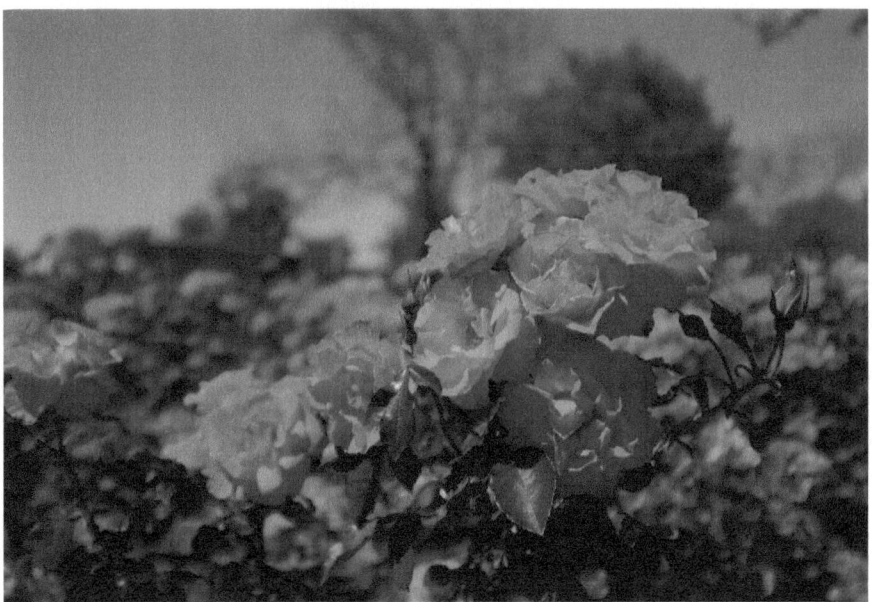

*Figure 11-7:* *Shot in the mid-afternoon sun on a warm, sunny day at 1/1000^th sec, F/2, ND "On", using an off-camera EF-X20 flash (attached via a cord) to create this rich ambient light balance.*

Unfortunately, in some X100 cameras, the ND Filter is not available in the Q-Menu, so the only way of gaining rapid access to toggle it as required, is by programming a/the Fn button. Indeed, in the X100S, I alternate the use of its single function button between ISO and ND filter accordingly.

---

*Tip:  **ND Impact on Flash** - Putting an ND filter in the light path also impacts on your use of flash. Adding three stops of ND between the subject and the sensor to cut ambient light, also cuts three stops of flash you used to light your subject with - or to put it another way, you need to use three-stops more flash to get the same job done as without the ND filter.*

***Tip #2:** You'll be more inclined to use the ND filter if you program it to a function button, or the Q-menu (where applicable).*

---

Now let's dive in and put all these elements together:

## RHSS IN ACTION

Let's establish the scenario in which you're most likely to want to put all these elements together.

The real benefit of your X100 series RHSS capability is its capacity to compete with ambient light. Let's be blunt. It's sunlight we're referring to – light which generally yields stark, flat, harshly lit images with unflattering shadows. Now though, we can use RHSS to balance the contribution of sunlight vs flash light, even whilst shooting in the noon-day sun.

Now though, armed with your X100/S/T and some strobes, you can operate in a wider range of lighting conditions, turning out acceptable, and even wonderfully inspiring, shallow depth of field (if you want) pictures in what would otherwise be lighting left exclusively to the purview of holiday snaps.

The most minimal kit you can use is the camera and a flash. The onboard flash will give you some scope. But you'll never really compete with strong ambient light with it. The EF-X20 accessory flash adds more scope. Off-camera strobes will take you even further. Here are some steps you might find useful in capturing RHSS shots:

- **Establish a composition.** Choose the subject, background, colours, light, and framing. Evaluate the scene.
- **Adjust aperture.** What do you want from your bokeh? (You don't usually hear that in the same context as using flash). This decision

establishes aperture. If you want everything in the background in focus (rivers, mountains, groups of people etc), use F/8 or more. If you want little of the background in focus, use F/2, or f/2.8 (determined by how much of your subject you want in focus).

- **Now adjust shutter speed** to expose for the background (as though the flash was not going to fire). At this stage, you are determining how dramatic you want the background to be. You can underexpose it, (presumably you are going through all this because you don't want to overexpose it) as much as you like. Of course, the huge benefit of RHSS is you can manage the level of background underexposure to suit your creative urge.

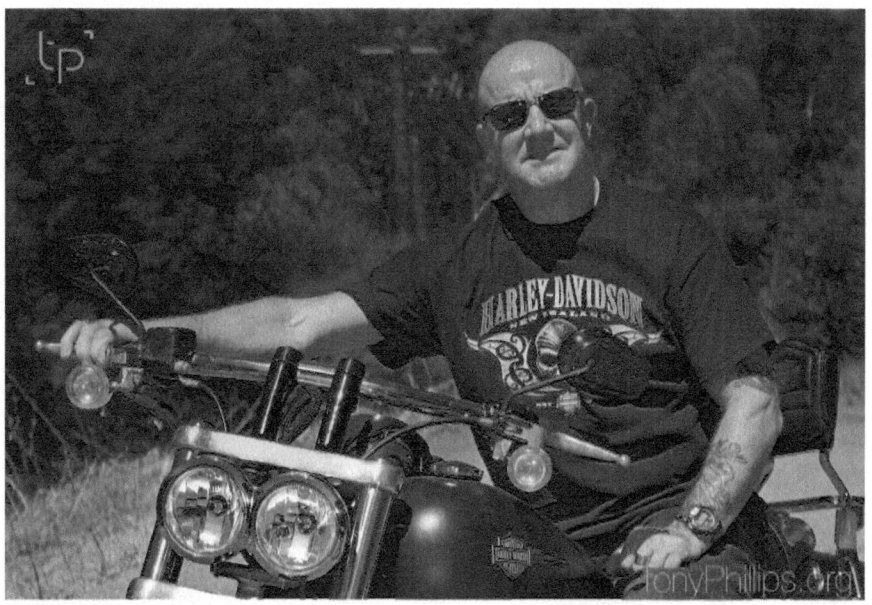

*Figure 11-8:* RHSS. Full summer sun. Steve was happy to show off his Harley. (1/2000th, f/2. GN 58 flash at ½ power on cable, ND filter on.)

- **Add in the ND filter** for more control over background exposure/shutter speed if you need it, allowing for your desired depth of field. This keeps you inside the allowable shutter vs aperture envelope and gives you wider aperture choices.

- **Establish flash contribution**. Use a flashmeter if you have one, to correctly expose for flash falling on the subject (only). No flashmeter? Use the techniques in the "manual flash" section to establish correct manual flash exposure. (EG: 1/8th power, 8ft flash distance, fire test shot, examine histogram. Repeat till perfect.
- **Fine tune the lighting ratio** between ambient and flash light.
- **Shoot away**. As always, shoot both portrait and landscape compositions - and look for other angles and ideas.

---

*Tip:* All flash units aren't equal when it comes to delivering their full flash output at the high shutter speeds you might use with X100 cameras.

This is a pretty big topic on its own. I suggest you consult the data sheet for your particular flash unit to discover the highest shutter speed at which it will deliver full (1/1) manual power. Of course, you can go higher than that shutter speed so long as you don't require a higher flash power setting than the flash is capable of delivering.

---

*Tip:* Usually when shooting with manual flash, **Shutter** speed controls **Ambient** light, and **Aperture** controls **Flash** (subject lighting). **(SAAF** mnemonic). Remember this, and it's easy to "dial" flash contribution up or down by increasing or decreasing aperture without leaving the camera (so long as you still have an acceptable depth of field with the chosen aperture setting, of course).

With RHSS though, you can retune your thinking somewhat. **Shutter** speed still controls **Ambient**, but you set **Aperture** to control **DOF** (depth of field) just as you would with non-flash shooting! I'm reticent to suggest **SAADOF** as a suitable mnemonic for RHSS – but if it helps...

---

> **Very Important TIP:** *If you're in manual exposure mode using RHSS, remember to* **manually alter ISO** *as well. With ISO on auto, your camera will use the one remaining automatic feature you've left to its discretion, to strive to make the exposure "normal" - which is not what you want at all. What you're doing with RHSS is not normal, and you'll get quite varied results using Auto ISO and RHSS.*
>
> *Since you probably have plenty of light, using the lowest native ISO available (ISO 200 – or 100 if you're shooting in FINE JPEG) will give the best results.*

## HAVING SAID ALL THAT...

Since *quality* of light is far more important than *quantity* of light, the high speed syncing capability of the X100 cameras gives you a powerful tool to take your creative desires further than before. With just a compact camera and a very small lighting kit (one or two external flash units, and umbrellas perhaps), you have a very capable setup to photograph outdoors, even on sunny days, turning out remarkable results with outstanding light quality. Surely a skill worth mastering.

As I said at the start of the chapter, this is the reason you really want an X100 series camera!

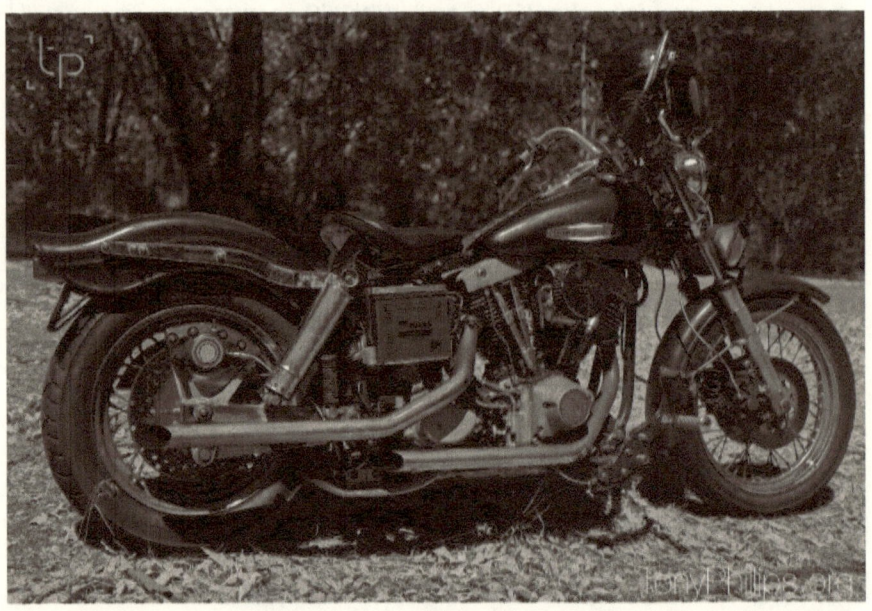

*Figure 11-9: Old Hogs never die! RHSS lifts Raylee's Harley from its parched surroundings. (Full summer sun, 1/1000$^{th}$, f/2. EF-X20 flash, ND filter.)*

# EPILOGUE

Congratulations on reaching this point!

I hope you enjoyed reading this book as much as I did writing it. Many people are daunted by manual flash, and the apparent limitations on using flash with the X-platform of cameras. But there is nothing to be daunted by – and I hope I've demonstrated that in this book, and encouraged you to experiment with lighting to broaden your range.

As you might imagine, books like this are a monumental effort. As mentioned at the time you bought this book, I'm an independent author and I have no advertising budget per se – instead, I rely solely on the enthusiastic recommendations people make to their friends and online. If you liked this book, if you feel it stands apart from other commercial-grade, corporate-backed, dryly written photography books, please speak up and let the world know about it! ☺ Here are some things you can do:

1. Feel free to visit any of the online forums mentioned in this chapter and tell people what you thought about it. Mention your skill level, mention what you liked (and even what you didn't like, if you must), and the links www.FriedmanArchives.com, & www.TonyPhillips.org .
2. Feel even freer to send me a testimonial via email at info@TonyPhillips.org. Parts of it may end up on the above websites or in future books.
3. Facebook and Twitter are great places to spread the word too!
4. The book is sold on Amazon and iTunes. Feel free to review it there.

Many thanks for committing your time. I'm glad to have shared this with you. I trust your interest in photographing interesting places in interesting ways gives you an expanded view of the wonderful world we live in, and hope that I've been able to contribute to your enjoyment.

# APPENDIX A – THE HISTOGRAM

Using the histogram is a viable way of determining correct exposure while shooting with manual flash. The following discussion covers all aspects of the histogram, including its use in manual flash photography.

## BRIGHTNESS

As mentioned early on in this book, cameras clearly do not see light the way *you and I* see light. Our eyes are a marvel current technology is nowhere near matching. I mean, how many times have you taken a picture and the outcome is way brighter, or way darker than *you* see the scene? Quite a few, right?

It's one of the challenges of being a photographer. You are creating images with light, with tools that just *don't see light the way you do*. So understanding *how* cameras see light, and *how* to get them to see light the way you want them to is part of the fun – and the challenge.

This all has to do with the notion of dynamic range. The dynamic range of your eyes, for instance, is about 30 stops of light! Digital camera sensors, on the other hand master only 8 stops or so. So no wonder you see what they don't "see".

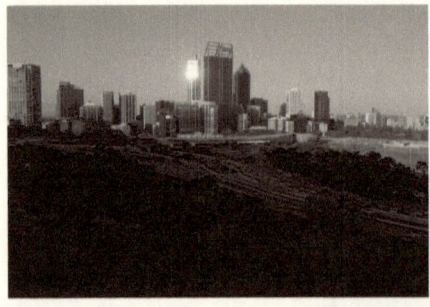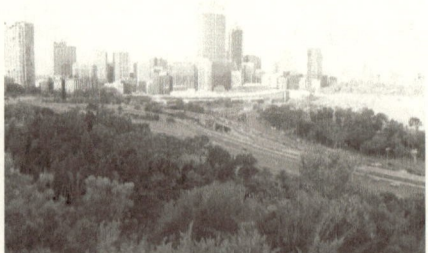

**Figure 1:** *Cameras can expose for light, or dark, but not both - the sky, or the foreground (in this case). What I saw when I took these pictures was neither of these scenes. Rather something more of a blend. You have to deliberately meter for the darks to get the image on the right.*

This is important to understand. If you metered for the scene in **Figure 1**, and you required 1/1000$^{th}$ of a second (shutter speed) for correct exposure of the brightest parts of the image, then 8 stops less than that means the darkest parts will only yield detail if you can properly expose them with 1/4 second shutter speed (8 stops away). That same 8 stop range for your eyes is a doddle. You see detail in the very brightest part of the image, and many, many stops below where your camera has given up and rendered everything black.

And the odd part is, while we can take multiple pictures and turn them into true HDR (high dynamic range) images, they seem quite fake to our eye. This clearly has to do with the way our brain processes these inputs.

This dynamic range difference between eye and camera is one of the reasons to use forced (fill) flash, even on a bright, sunny day (or especially on a bright sunny day), to lift detail in the shadow so you capture a scene more the way your eye sees it.

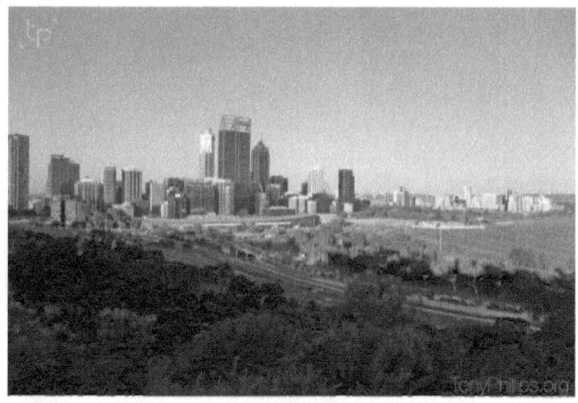

*Figure 2: This is an **attempt** to depict the scene as I saw it. And even this is not right. To add back the dark detail I could easily see simply makes the picture seem flat and bizarre.*

That is part of the reason the RHSS (real high speed sync) flash photography available with X100 series cameras appeals to me too. It gives me back richness and detail (the experience) I perceived I was having while I was in the scene shooting.

Of course, you can use the limited dynamic range of the sensor to artistic effect too, by creating silhouettes where your eye easily perceived detail – arriving at a pleasing image that in no way accurately reflects the scene you saw. See **Figure 3**.

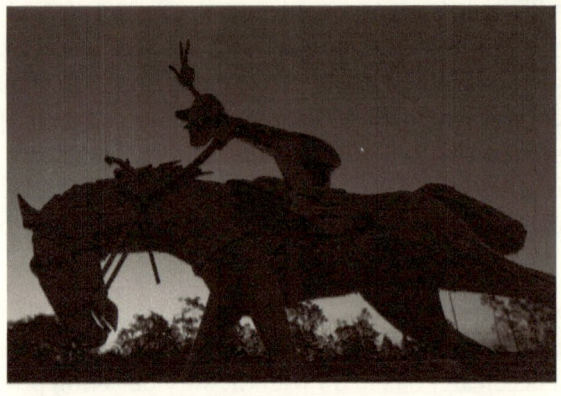

*Figure 3: Create silhouettes where there were none by turning limited dynamic range into art. You can spot meter, or simply winding down the exposure compensation might get you the result.*

But what about if you don't want to lose all the detail in the darks? Or you want to know you're capturing detail in a bride's dress, and not just rendering it a white detail-less mass.

Well, that's where the histogram will help you out.

## THE HISTOGRAM EXPOSED

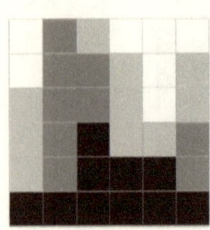

*Figure 4: This is a representation of Pixels in an image showing only their brightness.*

The Histogram shows you where brightness is distributed in a picture across the dynamic range of the camera's sensor. It shows therefore, if you are losing detail in whites and blacks.

To understand how a histogram works, examine the rudimentary "image" in **Figure 4**, and for a moment, imagine it represents only the *brightness* of pixels in an image.

If you graph this brightness in a histogram (a bar graph), you get the brightness distributed over the entire brightness range as shown in **Figure 5**. The height of each bar in the graph indicates the frequency of occurrence of a particular brightness, with most frequently-occurring brightnesses being taller, and least frequently-occurring being shortest (or non-existent). Brightest pixels are on the right side of the graph, and darkest on the left.

Of course, for some pictures this histogram might produce exactly the result you want, but for others, it could spell disaster. There is no "normal" histogram. It's just a tool. What's important is the understanding that if the graph is bunched up to the left, you have lots of dark pixels, and are losing detail in blacks because you have pushed exposure outside the dynamic range of the sensor. If they are up against the right side of the graph, you have lots of bright pixels, and are losing detail in the whites and are exceeding the limits of the sensor once more.

There are two histograms available to you in the camera. One on the shooting screen (assuming you have it turned on and one in playback (Detail Information screen).

When using the histogram to determine appropriate flash exposure as suggested in Chapter 8, you will be using the playback histogram after you take a test shot.

The following pages show some "decoded" histogram examples:

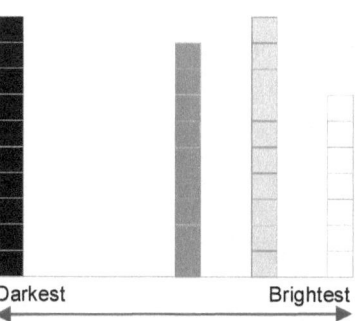

Darkest — Brightest

*Figure 5: In Figure 4 there are 10 black pixels, 9 mid-grey pixels, 10 grey pixels, and 7 white pixels. This is how that looks when you graph it as a histogram.*

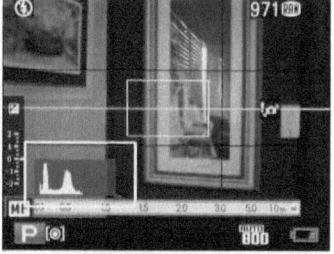

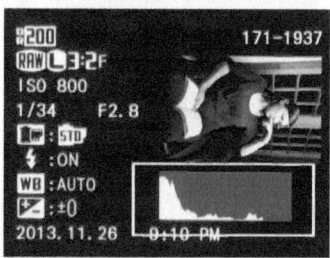

*Figure 6: Top: Histogram in live view shooting. Bottom: The "Detail Information" playback display shows a histogram of your shot.*

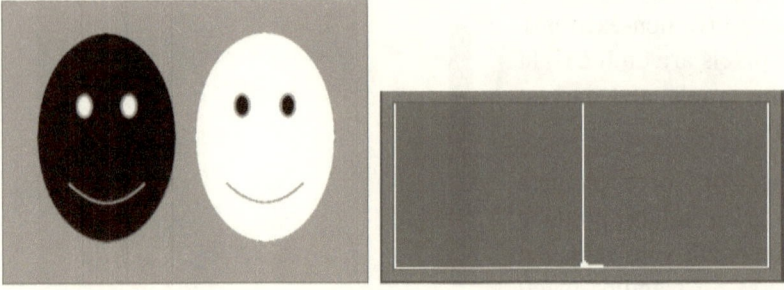

***Figure 7:*** *Let's start with something simple. This is what happens in the histogram (recall, it's a bar graph) with an an image comprised entirely of black, white, and grey.   Black on the left, white on the right, and grey in the middle.*

***Figure 8:***    *So what would you expect of an image which is all grey? Just one single spike indicates all the pixels are one brightness, and there's nothing anywhere else on the graph.*

***Figure 9:***      *When I photographed my grey backdrop it produced an image with texture, and a wider brightness range - with a histogram to match. Notice the light falloff across the image.*

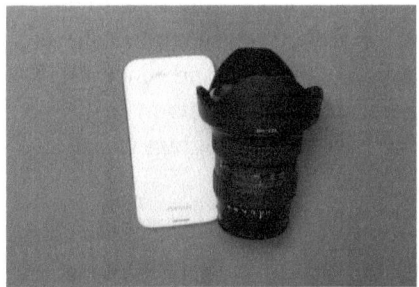 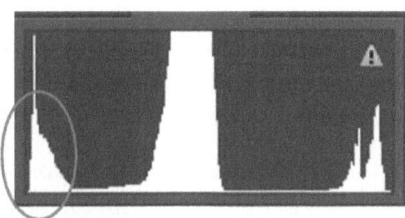

**Figure 10:** And this is what it looks like if you shoot something real. We still have the black spike on the left. Some dark grey indicated on the left too. The backdrop holds pride of place in the centre, and the less-than-white phone makes a showing on the right.

If you'd just taken this black/white image and were wondering if your blacks are blown out, a quick glance at the histogram shows you they aren't!

But enough of that. It's all grey! Let's look at some colour!

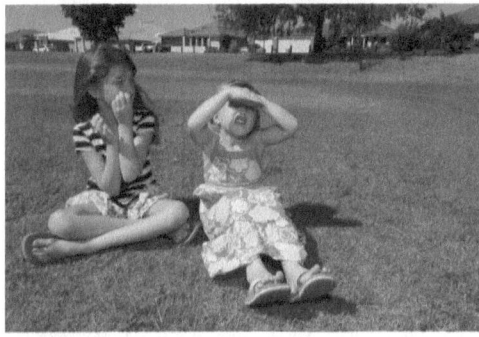 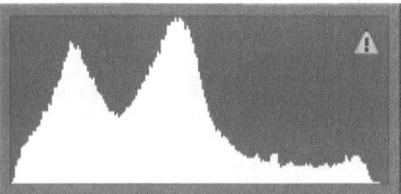

*Figure 11:* *Here's a nice little snapshot with a wide range of brightness across the histogram. The first "hump" represents darker tones like the trees and shadows. The second encompasses all the shades of green and all the other midtones, with the brighter skin, clothing and buildings stretching out toward the right.*

## THE HISTOGRAM AND MANUAL FLASH

In the preceding pages we looked at what a histogram is, and how to use it to ensure you have correct exposure (with, or without the use of flash) and are not losing details in either your blacks or whites. And since all X-platform cameras have a shooting histogram, you can do this in real time. Or you can take a test shot and inspect the playback histogram to achieve the same end.

Using the *playback* histogram to confirm correct exposure in manual flash photography (as suggested in Chapter 8), relies on the understanding we have developed so far. And it works equally well whether you are in a studio with backdrops and studio or portable flash lights (see **Figure 12**), or on location using portable flash to supplement your exposure (**Figure 13**).

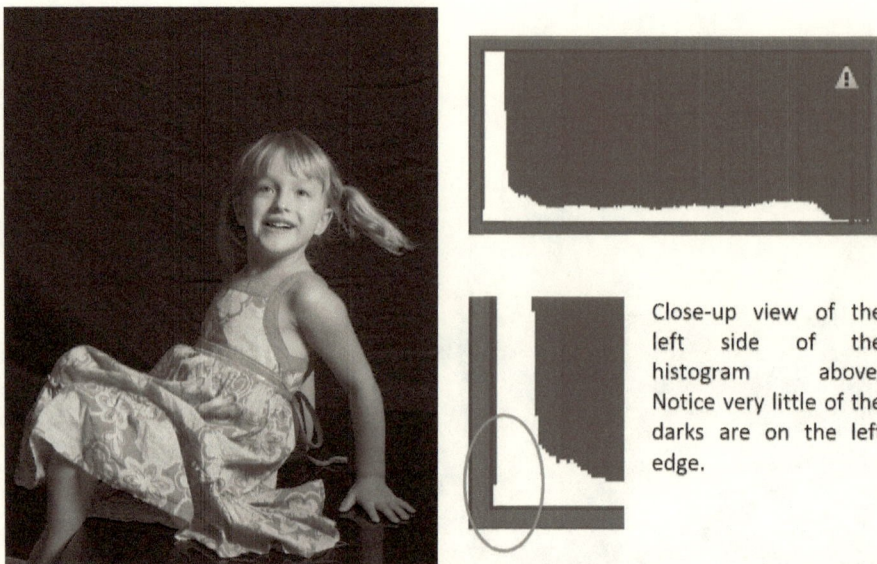

Close-up view of the left side of the histogram above. Notice very little of the darks are on the left edge.

*Figure 12: This is a studio image with a black background and a single diffused flash. The histogram shows what happens when there's more dark than bright in an image. Notice though that almost all the blacks are not so black that they bunch up on the left and lose detail. There's still detail in the blacks, and on a large monitor it is easy to see. Use the histogram to check flash exposure like this, and you'll have perfect exposure for this kind of shot.*

Indeed, using the procedures described in Chapter 8 to establish approximate starting distances for light placement, you can quickly shoot a test shot and examine the playback histogram as we have in **Figure 12**, and make power (or distance) adjustments to ensure you have proper flash exposure. This example concentrates on the left side of the histogram (underexposure), but given the preceding discussion, you can easily extrapolate this to see that if you had *too much power* on your flash, the image would possibly be overexposed, and the graph would bunch up on the right hand side.

While **Figure 13** is not a studio image, it illustrates this point admirably.

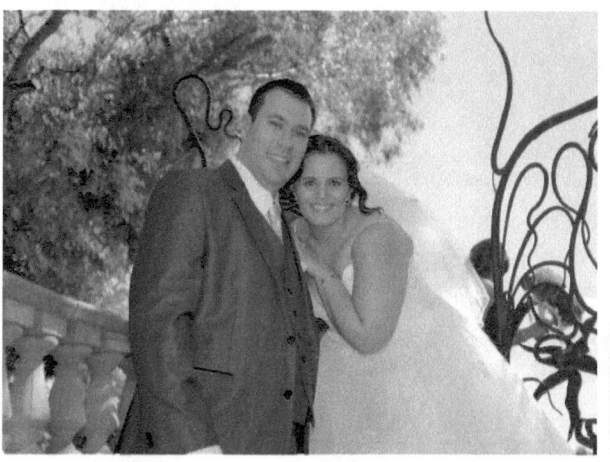
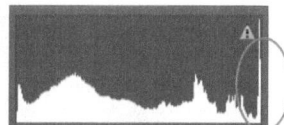

*Figure 13: Here's an image lit by both ambient **and** flash light. And it's one of those situations where you simply don't want to be wrong.*

A quick glance at the histogram show us we're losing a tiny bit of detail in the whitest part of the whites. Now given that a small portion of the dress is in sunlight, you might be OK to leave it be. Otherwise, dial exposure down a bit and flash up (to balance the exposure), and shoot again. Or better yet, do that, and shoot RAW, and you **know** you haven't lost anything in an image like this. (I would never **not** shoot a wedding in RAW. There's just too much at stake.)

---

*"**Blinking Exposed**: If any part of an image is overexposed or underexposed, those parts will "blink", making them easy to see in the Detailed Information playback screen. (Press the Disp button a number of times in playback mode to get to this screen).*

*The following demonstrates this blinking effect. I deliberately overexposed a shot of my PC screen, then photographed the two blinking states in playback mode (marked in yellow); and,*

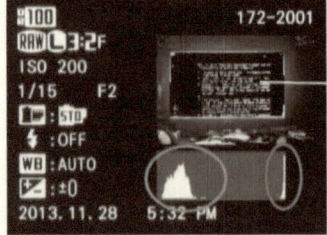 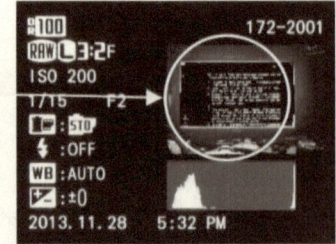

*the right-most part of the histogram (circled in red) that denotes the overexposure. Underexposure would show a similar spike on the left edge of the histogram. The green circle indicates the range of exposure for all the other junk on my desk ☺.*

*It's worth noting that even though this image is grossly overexposed, there is still some recoverable data in the highlights. And if you shoot in RAW, you'll have even more recovery overhead.*

---

# APPENDIX B – A CONDENSED GUIDE TO EXPOSURE

While this book is not designed to cover the basics of photography, it might be of value to some to have a refresher on the basics of exposure. To cover this material fully is another book in itself.


## PRIMARY EXPOSURE CONTROLS

This section exists as a prelude to an examination of the exposure controls which follow.

It's not meant to be an explanation of the basics of exposure. I'm going to assume you know what that's all about and are comfortable with semi-automatic Program AE **P** shooting, Aperture **A** , and Shutter **S** priority shooting, and Manual exposure **M** modes.

But to explain *what* the following exposure controls do/how they work, we need to touch on some essential information. So here goes…

In my camera books I talk a lot about metering for proper exposure, and adjusting exposure, but what controls exposure for any given availability of light?

Basically, there's ISO – the imaging sensor's sensitivity to light; there's the lens aperture – the size of the opening through which light must pass to reach the sensor; there's shutter speed – how long the shutter remains open to capture that light; and, for completeness, the exposure compensation dial – how much *YOU* want to over or underexpose the image from the camera's recommended exposure (which of course only matters when the camera is calculating some, or all of the exposure automatically in P, A, or S modes). Taken together, all these things act to control how much light gets through to the camera's sensor – and therefore how "properly" exposed the picture will be.

Of course, "proper" exposure is a bit misleading, because a picture can be underexposed (for example), and yet be exactly what you are looking for. And so, since camera's don't take pictures (people take pictures), understanding how to optimally control the exposure (the amount of light reaching the camera's sensor), will help you take the kind of pictures you want.

Let's look though at which controls affect each exposure mode. Remember, you can manually set ISO for these four exposure modes – including Auto ISO, which lets the camera make the ISO selection for you.

- In **P** Program exposure mode, *YOU* set the ISO, the camera modifies both shutter speed and aperture (f/stop) to create the exposure. This is called Program AE.
- In **A** Aperture exposure mode, *YOU* set the ISO and the aperture (f/stop) via the Aperture ring. The camera controls shutter speed.
- In **S** Shutter exposure mode *YOU* set the ISO and the shutter speed via the Shutter Speed Dial. The camera controls f/stop (aperture).

  You can tweak the camera's suggested exposure in any of these three semi-automatic modes using Exposure Compensation, or by using Program Shift. Both will be examined shortly.
- In **M** Manual exposure mode, *YOU* control ISO, shutter speed and aperture. The camera will still show you its suggestion for exposure along the bottom of the viewfinder, but it's relying on you to manually make the settings. Since they are semi-automatic tools only, neither Exposure Compensation nor Program Shift do anything in manual exposure mode.

  If you've been into photography for some time, you'll notice I arranged these exposure modes in the familiar **P A S M** acronym found on a dial somewhere on many cameras. I do this for familiarity only, not lamenting the absence of such a control in any way where the X100S is concerned. I very much like the intuitive arrangement between function and form as it's presented in this camera.

Let's turn our attention to the two exposure tweaking methods applicable to those first three semi-automatic exposure modes.

**Exposure Compensation** is available in the X-platform cameras via a dial. Whatever your camera suggests for exposure in either **P**, **A**, or **S** modes, can be overridden to some extent using the exposure compensation dial. Different "X" cameras have differing amounts of exposure compensation available to them.

**Program Shift** is a tad trickier to understand. But once mastered, will give you a trick or two up your sleeve. It comes with caveats though.

Program Shift is designed for Program AE shooting, and exists not to adjust the actual exposure of your intended image, but to change the way *setting that* exposure impacts on image composition.

What do I mean by that? Well, ignoring Exposure Compensation for a moment, if proper exposure at a given ISO is met by one combination of f/stop and shutter speed, it is also true that as long as they both add up to the *same exposure*, you can use a different combination of f/stop and shutter speed and still have "correct" exposure – right?

Of course you can. But since the camera is in automatic P mode, how do you do that? And more importantly, why would you want to?

As you know, f/stop controls depth of field (how deep the focus envelope is); and shutter speed controls how much you freeze/blur motion. And both of these are creative compositional tools.

If you want to freeze motion for example, you'd want a high shutter speed – perhaps 1/500$^{th}$ or even 1/1000$^{th}$ of a second depending on the actual speed of your subject. But if your camera recommends only 1/250$^{th}$ of a second in P mode, what do you do? You could switch to Shutter Exposure mode and set the desired shutter speed, or you could just Program Shift to it.

One more example before we go into how it's done and what the caveats are for using it: Let's say you wanted to create a really shallow depth of field (which you would get with f/2, say), but the camera wants to use f/5.6 – which is not anywhere near shallow enough for your intended outcome. As long as it's not too slow or too fast, you don't care too much what the shutter speed is, you're really concentrating on creating a blurred (bokeh) background. For the sake of our example, let's say the camera recommended 1/60$^{th}$ of a second shutter speed to achieve correct exposure. Using Program Shift you can quickly alter these exposure combinations to get what you want. Simply rotate the front command dial left or right, and watch the shutter speed and aperture numbers change in matched pairs to give you f/2 and 1/500$^{th}$ of a second, without changing the actual exposure at all. Now you have a shallow depth of field *and* an acceptable shutter speed, and will get that blurred background you were looking for.

***Caveats: You cannot use Program shift while you are using Auto ISO***, Auto DR (dynamic range) or the flash in TTL mode. I'm not sure why you cannot Program Shift in Auto ISO mode. This is not typical for high-end cameras. Curiously, the manual suggests you turn the camera off to cancel Program Shift. I just ignore it and go on to the next thing.

Let's now look at each of the exposure controls:

## SHUTTER SPEED

Controlling shutter speed does three things.

- Freezes the action in a moving scene,
- Blurs the action, giving the impression of movement,
- Reduces ambient light for RHSS (Real High Speed Sync) flash shots.

Set the shutter speed too low, and you need to place the camera on a stable surface (or tripod) to avoid blur from camera shake.

Once you know the effect you want to create, you can rotate the Shutter Speed dial to your desired choice. Leave the Aperture ring in "A" mode position, and you're in Shutter priority shooting ( S ) mode. Just be sure not to exceed the maximum shutter sync speed for flash (1/180th in interchangeable lens X-platform cameras, and 1/2000th in leaf shutter "X" cameras) if you are using flash as either your main, or fill light.

Adjust shutter speed up or down from the dialed-in setting using the appropriate Controller.

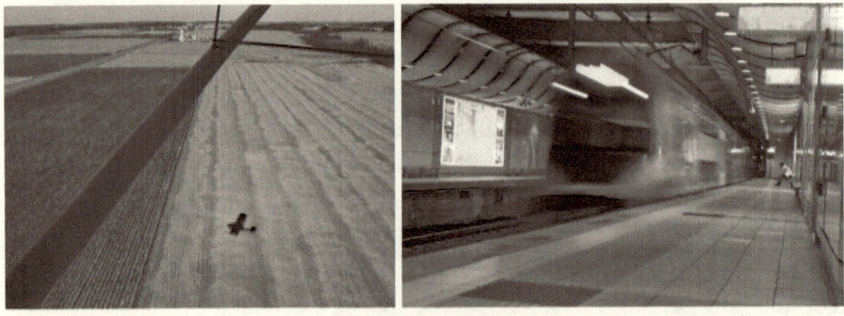

**Left**: *Freeze action with fast shutter speeds, or* **Right**: *blur action with slower shutter speeds.*

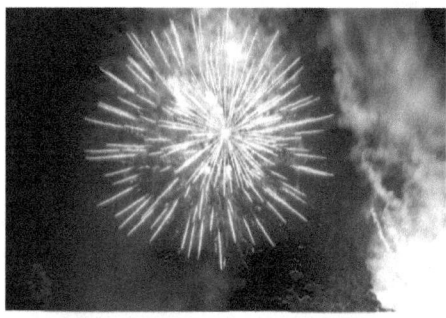 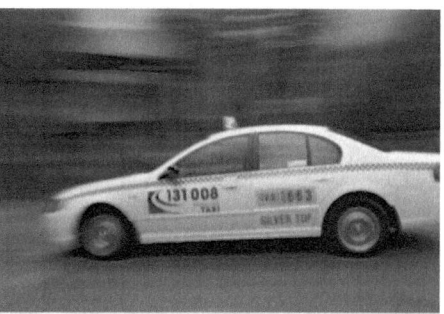

**Left**: *Use a slow shutter speed with a stable camera to blur all sorts of action.* **Right**: *Slowing the shutter and panning the camera while the shutter is open, will blur the background!*

## APERTURE (F/STOPS)

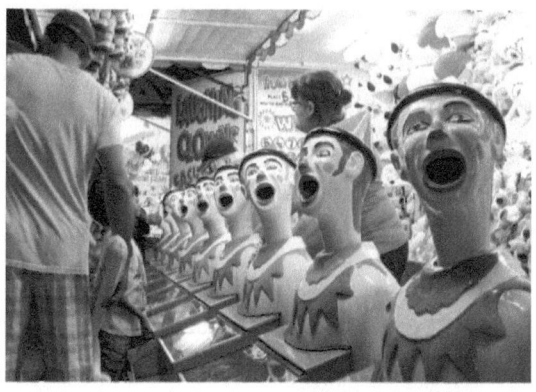

*Sometimes you want a wide Depth of Field (envelope), and a small f/stop (around f/16) is the answer. (Though f/8 was all it took for this image.)*

Aperture (also known as "F/stop") means "the lens opening". The size of the opening not only controls how much light reaches the sensor, it also determines how wide the Depth of Field (in-focus) envelope is surrounding the focus point. Your Fujifilm camera has an outstanding Focus Indicator which shows both the focus point and this DOF envelope.

The aperture blades (built into the lens) act somewhat like the iris in your eye. When it's dark, your iris opens wide to let in light. This is akin to setting large f/stops (f/1.2, 2.8). Counterintuitively, the numbering might seem to indicate a small opening, but it's really the opposite. With large apertures (smaller numbers), you have a tiny DOF envelope. Which means not much besides what you are focused on is going to be in focus.

Large numbers like f/8, f/16, indicate smaller aperture openings (like the iris in your eye in bright sunlight). The larger the number, the deeper your DOF envelope – so quite a bit (both before and behind your subject) will be in focus.

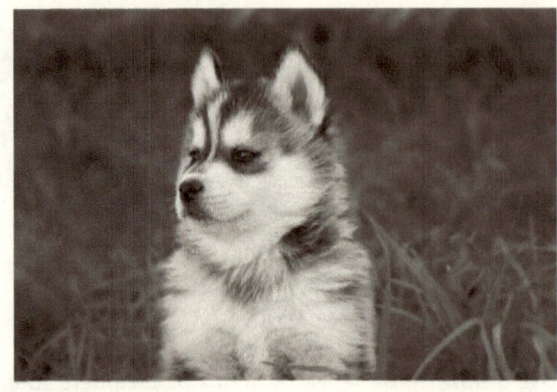

*Sometimes you want a shallow Depth of Field envelope to create a blurred background which will highlight your subject. A large f/stop (around f/2.0) will do this for you.*

Once you know the effect you want to create, you can rotate the Aperture ring on the lens to your desired choice. Leave the Shutter Speed dial in "**A**" position, and you're in Aperture priority shooting ( **A** ) mode.

Depending on your "X" camera/lens, you can now adjust aperture up or down from the dialed-in setting using the controller wheel or aperture ring.

## ISO

ISO used to mean how sensitive a film was to light. Now it means the same, though the "film" is the imaging sensor. The higher the ISO, the more sensitive it becomes – though it becomes noisier too.

Shutter speed, ISO and Aperture all affect image exposure. When you adjust one, you must change at least one of the others to compensate.

## EXPOSURE VARIABLES – THE TRADEOFFS

High shutter speeds:
- freeze motion
- let in less light (darken picture)

Low shutter speeds:
- blur motion

- let in more light (lighten picture)

Small apertures (large numbers):
- increase what's in focus (wide depth)
- let in less light (darken picture)

Large apertures (small numbers):
- decrease what's in focus (shallow depth)
- let in more light (lighten picture)

Low ISO:
- decreases sensor sensitivity to light (darkens picture)
- has lowest image noise

High ISO:
- increases sensor sensitivity to light (lightens picture)
- has higher image noise

The relationship between these three variables is pictured below:

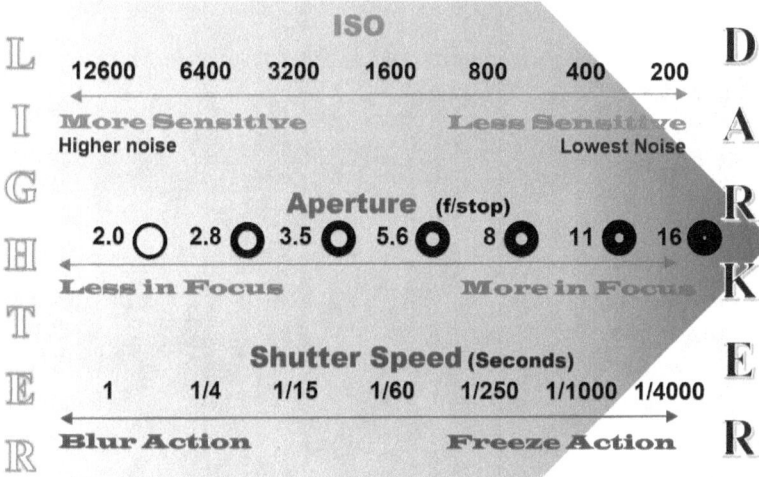

*The relationships between ISO, Aperture and Shutter Speed. Altering any one of these impacts on exposure requiring an adjustment in at least **one** of the others.*

*Tip:* Having difficulty calculating the relationship between exposure variables? As they say, there's an App for that. If you have a smartphone, you can download an App that will take the heavy lifting out of it for you.

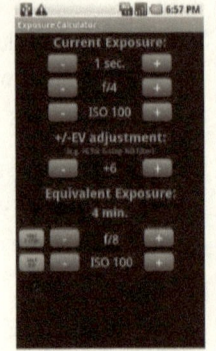

On Android, "Exposure Calculator" by RAWAPPS is simple and free, and doesn't (seem) to infest your phone with spyware or advertising. I've included a screen shot to show you how simple this is to use.

There are similar Apps for iPhones, of course.

Here's the android link:

(*https://play.google.com/store/apps/developer?id=RAWapps* )

---

*Advanced Tip*: Once you appreciate that there is a depth of field envelope, **where** to focus becomes an interesting question. There's a photo-graphic technique known as hyper-focal distance calculation. It's a trick to get what **you** want in focus by using the entire depth of the DOF envelope to your advantage. Once you know how **deep** the envelope is at your chosen aperture setting, simply refocus on something that will "move" your DOF envelope to surround everything **you** want in focus.

I was walking Southbank (Melbourne), and decided to take this picture to make into a monochrome. I was thinking boardwalks and old-world gas lamps at the time. Vitals are: handheld, 1/8s @ f/2.8 - meaning a narrow DOF. So where do you focus? I knew the buildings were too far away to resolve sharply no matter what, and 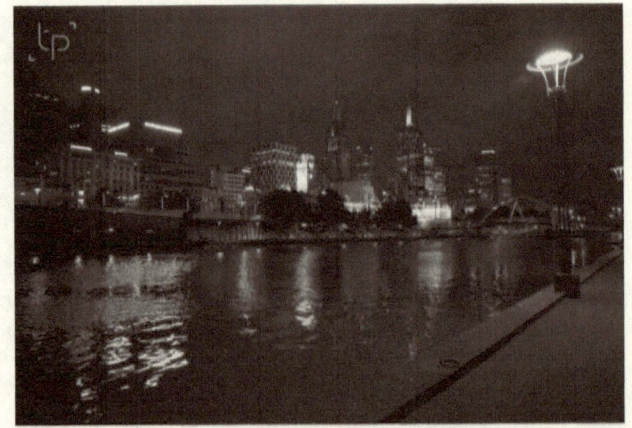 decided the water and the path near me should be in focus. So knowing HFD, I focused just past the eye-bolt in the foreground, then re-composed the shot. This made the path all the way to the bottom of the frame sharp (enough), giving an impression of sharpness to the entire image. Point at the buildings though, and the path would be indistinct.

# APPENDIX C - ADDITIONAL RESOURCES – GO FURTHER

## BUT WAIT! THERE'S MORE!

I hope this book has whet your appetite some for what you can do with flash. If you'd like to follow this further – to be inspired, to learn more, to create stirring images, *and* have some fun with off-camera (wireless) flash, spend some quality time at www.strobist.com.

From the website:

*"Think of Strobist as a lighting idea bank, run by and for the most enthusiastic DSLR photographers. Our goal is to exchange ideas with other shooters and post many different lighting techniques - using real-world assignments as examples."*

Of course, photography is a big subject. It's part art, part technical, and part mumbo jumbo ☺. Some people are drawn to the art. Some to the technical wizardry (and others to the mumbo jumbo!).

In this book I've tried to provide information, insight, and inspiration. It's all an ongoing journey with new and interesting things to experiment with. There's lots of help along the way. Photographers are generally an open bunch, freely sharing knowledge and experience. There are many internet resources that can help, and I've cobbled some of these together.

## GENERAL INTERNET RESOURCES

### FORUMS, CAMERA/LENS REVIEWS, IMAGES ONLINE, & MORE

There is a vast array of resources on the Internet where you can ask questions, learn from the experience of others, and even post pictures and get feedback. (It's possible you may have even heard about this book via one of them!)

- www.DPReview.com – Well known for detailed camera and lens reviews and expansive forums. There's a lot on "X" system cameras.

- www.steves-digicams.com (Steve's Digicams) – Similar to DPReview. Try both.

- www.imaging-resource.com – Another site akin to DPReview. Detailed camera reviews.

- www.Photodo.com – Offers fairly detailed evaluations of lenses.

- www.DxOMark.com – DXOMark has an in-depth testing methodology to rate RAW files across popular camera manufacturers (colour depth, dynamic range, ISO noise levels). DXO commercially sells software designed to correct lens flaws. Of course, *you* already have LMO ☺ (which sadly doesn't apply to RAW files).

- www.Fujix-forum.com (Fujix forum) – Everything Fujifilm! Articles, news, rumours, forums.

- http://luminous-landscape.com (Luminous Landscape) – Huge resource: Outstanding images. Video tutorials for sale. Articles, tutorials and forums.

- www.Photo.net (Photo.net) – a web-based photo discussion board focused on images over brands. Outstanding for hosting and sharing images.

- www.Flickr.com (Flickr) – Upload your images for all to see.

- www.FriedmanArchives.com (The Friedman Archives) – A great stock image website from the publisher of this book. Many other photography ebooks for sale.

- www.TonyPhillips.org (Author site) – Stock images, Seminars and other books.

## PUBLISHER OFFERINGS OF INTEREST

Friedman Archives (publisher of many of my photography books) offers other stimulating material you might be interested in.

### 25 WAYS TO "WOW!" E-BOOKLET

Now that you've become familiar with all of your camera's bells and whistles, I invite you to expand your mind - the right side of your brain, to be specific - and unleash some of its creative forces. Creativity, above all else, is really what makes great photography.

Check out the "25 Ways to 'Wow!'" e-booklet, a collection of 25 ideas and additional compositional rules designed to get your creative juices flowing and to help you take the kinds of pictures that make people say "Wow!" (the goal of every photographer!). It is available for USD $5.95 as an instantly-downloadable .pdf file.

*"25 Ways To Wow!"* Covers:

- What many National Geographic photographers do that you'll swear is unethical
- The "inner game" mindsets used by all the photographic masters
- The simple things that differentiate "art" from mere snapshots
- At least a dozen additional compositional rules (over and above what appears in this book)
- Ways to salvage low light conditions and turn them into memorable shots
- Three simple steps to making every shot outstanding

And much more!

## *ADVANCED TOPICS 2*

Another e-booklet (also instantly downloadable) delves into more technical interests that lie outside the purview of this book.

*"Advanced Topics 2"* Covers:

- Filters - what's useful, what's obsolete
- Color Space, Bit Depth, and ICC Profiles Explained
- Bird and Wildlife Photography
- Macro Photography
- Long-term Archiving of Gigabytes of Information
- Low-light Sports Photography
- The Basics of High Dynamic Range (HDR) Imaging (the old fashioned way to do it. It was uphill both ways!).

Both e-booklets can be purchased and downloaded by visiting www.FriedmanArchives.com/ebooks.

*BOOKS ON OTHER CAMERAS*

Friedman Archives offers a ton of books on other high-end cameras – mostly Fujifilm, Sony and Minolta, but the collection is steadily growing and expanding across various brands like Olympus). You can see the entire range at www.FriedmanArchives.com/ebooks

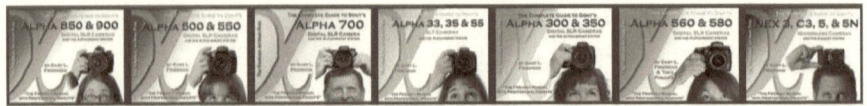

## CAMERACRAFT MAGAZINE

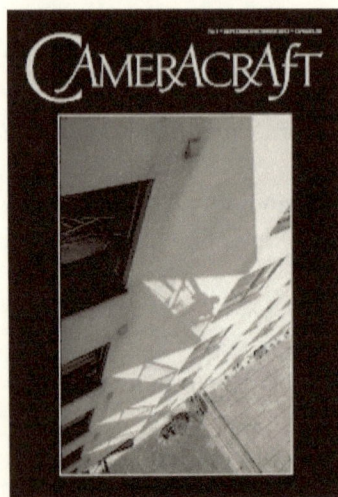

For as long as I can remember, the vast majority of "Popular" photography magazines simply serve as a vehicle for their advertisers.

Now things have changed. You might like to check out this outstanding magazine from legendary publisher David Kilpatrick.

If you're interested, here's a subscription link:

http://friedmanarchives.com/cameracraft

## WAYS TO 'WOW!' WITH WIRELESS FLASH

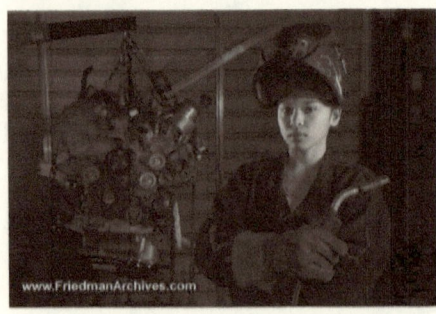

Just as there is no substitute for good focusing, there's no substitute for good light! That's why learning wireless flash is the best investment you can make in taking your photography to the next level. Take the plunge and learn to use this essential tool the non-intimidating way!

http://friedmanarchives.com/WWWF

## HIGH-IMPACT PHOTOGRAPHY SEMINARS

Want to expand your photographic insights and skills to the next level and get the most out of your camera? Both Gary Friedman (owner of Friedman Archives) and Tony Phillips (author), offer seminars designed to help you easily create "Wow!" shots, *and* gain an intuitive understanding of the technical aspects of photography which will help you get there.

Our seminars are different from any photography seminar that has come before, and have inspired a legion of beginners and 30-year-shooting-veterans alike to be more creative with their photography, learning both what is important for those "Wow!" type shots, *and* demystifying the technical aspects which can sometimes hold you back. It's fun, friendly and supportive.

Here are some of things you'll learn from this 2-day seminar:

**Day 1** ("The Creativity Day", or "The camera can do quite a bit by itself. This is all about creativity and light and things that only humans can do!")

- How to take great pictures with ANY camera!
- The secrets of outstanding travel photography
- The difference between snapshots and photographs (and why both are important)
- How to "see" light, and making the most of available light
- The "inner game" mindsets used by all the photographic masters
- Compositional rules derived from the world of fine art
- Hands-on experience with wireless flash
- How quality of light can affect emotion
- In-class exercises for creativity and composition.
- Pixel Peeping and Giant Enlargements – how many megapixels do you need?

**Day 2** ("The Technical Stuff")

- The four variables of exposure
- The three types of metering, and when to use them.
- How your exposure meter thinks.
- Color balance and Human Perception
- The benefits and drawbacks of RAW mode
- How to avoid horrific .jpg compression artifacts
- Print vs. screen resolution

- The most-useful Post-processing functions

There are also ample exercises allowing you to become more familiar with your camera, and experiment with various features. Interestingly, though the seminars were originally designed for beginners, many 30-year veterans of photography have exclaimed how much they learned and how their creativity was re-energized.

***The Friedman Archives Photography Seminars***, and ***TonyPhillips Love-Learn Photography Seminars*** are a wonderful way to help you get the most out of your camera, and invigorate your creative spirit. More information (including cities and schedules) can be found at:

> www.TonyPhillips.org/seminars and
> www.FriedmanArchives.com/seminars

Come visit the sites and register your interest in having a seminar in your city! If you're a member of a photo club you can get us there even faster. These seminars run all over the world, wherever there's demand.

# INDEX